Red Hat Enterprise Linux Server Cookbook

Over 60 recipes to help you build, configure, and orchestrate RHEL 7 Server to make your everyday administration experience seamless

William Leemans

BIRMINGHAM - MUMBAI

Red Hat Enterprise Linux Server Cookbook

First published: December 2015

Production reference: 1151215

Published by Packt Publishing Ltd.
Livery Place
35 Livery Street
Birmingham B3 2PB, UK.

ISBN 978-1-78439-201-7

www.packtpub.com

Credits

Author

William Leemans

Reviewers

Kyung Huh

Marcus Young

Commissioning Editor

Kunal Parikh

Acquisition Editor

Reshma Raman

Content Development Editor

Arshiya Ayaz Umer

Technical Editor

Siddhesh Ghadi

Copy Editor

Shruti Iyer

Project Coordinator

Shipra Chawhan

Proofreader

Safis Editing

Indexer

Monica Ajmera Mehta

Graphics

Disha Haria

Production Coordinator

Conidon Miranda

Cover Work

Conidon Miranda

About the Author

William Leemans has over 20 years of experience in the IT industry in various positions and supporting several environments.

In 2005, he started his own consulting company, Critter BVBA, in the hope of offering open source solutions to his customers, who are mainly enterprises.

In 2010, William started supporting Red Hat products full time with the Federal Police, Belgium. Since then, he has moved on to support Red Hat products at Proximus and now Euroclear.

William is a strong open source supporter and contributes where he can. He has a couple of projects running at GitHub (`https://github.com/bushvin`). During the course of writing this book, William recertified himself as a Red Hat Certified Engineer, hoping to one day become a Red Hat Certified Architect.

When he's not tapping away at the keyboard of his laptop, William likes to play around with his two young children, listen to rock music (Foo Fighters, AC/DC, and Queens of the Stone Age are some of his favorites), and devising complicated and intricate plots for the stories that he runs at his biweekly roleplaying sessions with his friends.

Thank you, Caroline, my dear wife, for being my soul mate, supporting me during this lengthy process, and giving me the space, time, and motivation to see this to the end.

Thanks, Mom, Dad, and Fre, for your relentless and unwavering belief in me and support, regardless of my rebellious antics.

Thank you, Tim, for telling me that I should get into computers when you did. I wouldn't know where I would've ended up if you hadn't!

Thank you, Gilad, for being the friend I need in my darkest hours and my most joyous moments!

Thank you, Wednesday Guys, for the support and fun. Koeken troef!

Thank you, Dag, for taking me on to yet another rather interesting adventure in my life called Red Hat.

About the Reviewers

Kyung Huh is a senior consultant at Red Hat based in Korea. He is a Red Hat Certified Architect. Kyung has worked with Linux and open source software for more than 16 years as an instructor and consultant. He has a lot of experience in Linux environments and building virtualization and cloud infrastructures, such as Red Hat Enterprise Virtualization and Red Hat OpenStack Platform, on the field. Kyung also reviewed *Hybrid Cloud Management with Red Hat CloudForms* and *Getting Started with Red Hat Enterprise Virtualization* by Packt Publishing.

Marcus Young recently graduated with a degree in computer science and mathematics before getting involved in system administration and DevOps. He currently works in software automation using open source tools and technologies. Marcus' hobbies include playing ice hockey and making home-brewed beer. He also enjoys hardware projects based on microcontrollers and single-board computers.

Marcus authored *Implementing Cloud Design Patterns for AWS, Packt Publishing*, as well.

www.PacktPub.com

Support files, eBooks, discount offers, and more

For support files and downloads related to your book, please visit www.PacktPub.com.

Did you know that Packt offers eBook versions of every book published, with PDF and ePub files available? You can upgrade to the eBook version at www.PacktPub.com and as a print book customer, you are entitled to a discount on the eBook copy. Get in touch with us at service@packtpub.com for more details.

At www.PacktPub.com, you can also read a collection of free technical articles, sign up for a range of free newsletters and receive exclusive discounts and offers on Packt books and eBooks.

https://www2.packtpub.com/books/subscription/packtlib

Do you need instant solutions to your IT questions? PacktLib is Packt's online digital book library. Here, you can search, access, and read Packt's entire library of books.

Why Subscribe?

- ▶ Fully searchable across every book published by Packt
- ▶ Copy and paste, print, and bookmark content
- ▶ On demand and accessible via a web browser

Free Access for Packt account holders

If you have an account with Packt at www.PacktPub.com, you can use this to access PacktLib today and view 9 entirely free books. Simply use your login credentials for immediate access.

Table of Contents

Preface

Gnu/Linux is the most important OS in the data center but how do you leverage it? How do you maintain and contain it? Many Gnu/Linux distributions try to answer these questions, but not all succeed. Red Hat Enterprise Linux is one that does answer these questions.

The next question is how do you, as a system administrator, manage a RHEL infrastructure? How do you deploy not just one system, but many? How do you make sure that it is secure and up to date? How can you monitor system components?

It may seem odd to you, but as a Red Hat Certified Engineer, I prefer the "lazy" approach—not as in "I can't be bothered," but as in "I like to do something once and do it good the first time and spend the rest of my time doing fun stuff."

In this book, I try to show you how to set up and configure systems, mainly by providing useful information to automate the setup, configuration, and management. This also explains the lack of the use of a GUI in this book. I'll be honest with you; I couldn't live without one on my laptop or desktop, but I do not believe servers should have a GUI. GUI-based applications tend not to have command-line counterparts, and I solemnly believe that if you cannot install, configure, manage, and maintain a piece of software through a script, it does not belong on a server.

This book does not pretend to be the de facto answer to all questions (that would be 42), but I do hope that you will learn something new and that, in turn, you will put this knowledge to good use. Remember, with great power, comes great responsibility!

What this book covers

Chapter 1, *Working with KVM Guests*, will not start by installing a basic RHEL system. It will start by introducing you to KVM if you don't already know it. You'll learn how to install and configure the KVM host and manage your KVM guests (the VMs). It will discuss the basics of adding resources on the fly, moving disks, and even moving the entire guest to another KVM host.

Chapter 2, Deploying RHEL "En Masse", will explore the ways of installing a RHEL system, introducing you to kickstart deployments, which are used to streamline automated system installs. If you want to orchestrate your environment, this chapter will lay out the basics for you to build on.

Chapter 3, Configuring Your Network, will explore `NetworkManager` tools to manage your network configuration, including advanced topics such as VLANs, link aggregation, and bridges. It will show you how to leverage its command-line tools to automate your system's network configuration during its deployment or afterwards, when all is installed.

Chapter 4, Configuring Your New System, will explain how to configure the basics, such as log retention, time, and your boot environment. It will also introduce you to the new systemd, which is SysVinit's replacement, and to monitoring and managing your services.

Chapter 5, Using SELinux, will give you an overview, but a brief one, on how to manage and troubleshoot SELinux on your system. SELinux is becoming more and more important in today's world because of its security implementation, and it's better to know about it than to just turn it off because you can't handle it.

Chapter 6, Orchestrating with Ansible, will tell you all about Ansible, which was recently bought by Red Hat. It will show you how to create simple playbooks that easily deploy new systems and how to manage your system's configuration.

Chapter 7, Puppet Configuration Management, will show you how to set up and configure Puppet. It will also give you a peek at its configuration management capacities.

Chapter 8, Yum and Repositories, will take a look at yum repositories, how you can create your own mirrors of the existing (Red Hat) repositories, and how to leverage it to keep your RHEL environment up to date without breaking a sweat.

Chapter 9, Securing RHEL 7, will take security configuration and auditing problems a bit further. We'll explore how to configure setting up centralized secure authentication and privilege escalation. It will show you how you can operate a system that appears to be "hung" and trace the root cause of the event.

Chapter 10, Monitoring and Performance Tuning, will show you the basics of easy performance tuning and how to monitor your system's resources.

What you need for this book

The only thing you'll need for the recipes in this book is the Red Hat Enterprise Linux 7 Installation DVD, for which you can download an evaluation license from `https://access.redhat.com/downloads`. All software used in this book is either available through the RHEL media or the yum repositories specified in the recipes.

Who this book is for

This book is for the system administrators who want to learn about the new RHEL version and features that are included for management or certification purposes. Although this book provides a lot of information to get your Red Hat Certified System Administrator and/or Red Hat Certified Engineer certifications, it is by far a complete guide to get either!

To get the most of this book, you should have a working knowledge of the basic (RHEL) system administration and management tools.

Sections

In this book, you will find several headings that appear frequently (Getting ready, How to do it, How it works, There's more, and See also).

To give clear instructions on how to complete a recipe, we use these sections as follows:

Getting ready

This section tells you what to expect in the recipe, and describes how to set up any software or any preliminary settings required for the recipe.

How to do it...

This section contains the steps required to follow the recipe.

How it works...

This section usually consists of a detailed explanation of what happened in the previous section.

There's more...

This section consists of additional information about the recipe in order to make the reader more knowledgeable about the recipe.

See also

This section provides helpful links to other useful information for the recipe.

Conventions

In this book, you will find a number of text styles that distinguish between different kinds of information. Here are some examples of these styles and an explanation of their meaning.

Code words in text, database table names, folder names, filenames, file extensions, pathnames, dummy URLs, user input, and Twitter handles are shown as follows: "We can include other contexts through the use of the `include` directive."

A block of code is set as follows:

```
node /^www[0-9]+\.critter\.be$/ {
}
node /^repo[0-9]+\.critter\.be$/ {
}
```

Any command-line input or output is written as follows:

```
~]# yum install -y /tmp/puppetlabs-release-el-7.noarch.rpm
```

New terms and **important words** are shown in bold. Words that you see on the screen, for example, in menus or dialog boxes, appear in the text like this: "Clicking the **Next** button moves you to the next screen."

Warnings or important notes appear in a box like this.

Tips and tricks appear like this.

Reader feedback

Feedback from our readers is always welcome. Let us know what you think about this book—what you liked or disliked. Reader feedback is important for us as it helps us develop titles that you will really get the most out of.

To send us general feedback, simply e-mail feedback@packtpub.com, and mention the book's title in the subject of your message.

If there is a topic that you have expertise in and you are interested in either writing or contributing to a book, see our author guide at www.packtpub.com/authors.

Customer support

Now that you are the proud owner of a Packt book, we have a number of things to help you to get the most from your purchase.

Downloading the color images of this book

We also provide you with a PDF file that has color images of the screenshots/diagrams used in this book. The color images will help you better understand the changes in the output. You can download this file from `https://www.packtpub.com/sites/default/files/downloads/RedHatEnterpriseLinuxServerCookbook_ColorImages.pdf`.

Errata

Although we have taken every care to ensure the accuracy of our content, mistakes do happen. If you find a mistake in one of our books—maybe a mistake in the text or the code—we would be grateful if you could report this to us. By doing so, you can save other readers from frustration and help us improve subsequent versions of this book. If you find any errata, please report them by visiting `http://www.packtpub.com/submit-errata`, selecting your book, clicking on the **Errata Submission Form** link, and entering the details of your errata. Once your errata are verified, your submission will be accepted and the errata will be uploaded to our website or added to any list of existing errata under the Errata section of that title.

To view the previously submitted errata, go to `https://www.packtpub.com/books/content/support` and enter the name of the book in the search field. The required information will appear under the **Errata** section.

Piracy

Piracy of copyrighted material on the Internet is an ongoing problem across all media. At Packt, we take the protection of our copyright and licenses very seriously. If you come across any illegal copies of our works in any form on the Internet, please provide us with the location address or website name immediately so that we can pursue a remedy.

Please contact us at `copyright@packtpub.com` with a link to the suspected pirated material.

We appreciate your help in protecting our authors and our ability to bring you valuable content.

Questions

If you have a problem with any aspect of this book, you can contact us at `questions@packtpub.com`, and we will do our best to address the problem.

Working with KVM Guests

1

In this chapter, we will cover the following recipes:

- ▶ Installing and configuring a KVM
- ▶ Configuring resources
- ▶ Building VMs
- ▶ Adding CPUs on the fly
- ▶ Adding RAM on the fly
- ▶ Adding disks on the fly
- ▶ Moving disks to another storage
- ▶ Moving VMs
- ▶ Backing up your VM metadata

Introduction

This book will attempt to show you how to deploy RHEL 7 systems without too much of a hassle. As this book is written with automation in mind, I will emphasize on command-line utilities rather than elaborating on its GUI counterparts, which are useless for automation.

This chapter explains how to build and manage KVM guests using the libvirt interface and various tools built around it. It will provide a brief overview on how to set up a KVM on RHEL and manage its resources. The setup provided in this overview is far from the ready enterprise as it doesn't provide any redundancy, which is generally required in enterprises. However, the recipes provided are relevant in enterprise setups as the interface stays the same. Most of the time, you will probably use a management layer (such as RHEV or oVirt), which will make your life easier in managing redundancy.

Libvirt is the API between the user and the various virtualization and container layers that are available, such as KVM, VMware, Hyper-V, and Linux Containers. Check `https://libvirt.org/drivers.html` for a complete list of supported hypervisors and container solutions.

As most tasks performed need to be automated in the end, I tend not to use any graphical interfaces as these do not allow an easy conversion into script. Hence, you will not find any recipes in this chapter involving a graphical interface. These recipes will primarily focus on `virsh`, the libvirt management user interface that is used to manage various aspects of your KVM host and guests. While a lot of people rely on the edit option of `virsh`, it doesn't allow you to edit a guest's configuration in real time. Editing your guest's XML configuration in this way will require you to shut down and boot your guest for the changes to take effect. A reboot of your guest doesn't do the trick as the XML configuration needs to be completely reread by the guest's instance in order for it to apply the changes. Only a fresh boot of the guest will do this.

The `virsh` interface is also a shell, so by launching `virsh` without any commands, you will enter the libvirt management shell. A very interesting command is `help`. This will output all the available commands grouped by keyword. Each command accepts the `--help` argument to show a detailed list of the possible arguments, and their explanation, which you can use.

Installing and configuring a KVM

This recipe covers the installing of virtualization tools and packages on RHEL 7.

By default, a RHEL 7 system doesn't come with a KVM or libvirt preinstalled. This can be installed in three ways:

- ▸ Through the graphical setup during the system's setup
- ▸ Via a kickstart installation
- ▸ Through a manual installation from the command line

For this recipe, you should know how to install packages using yum, and your system should be configured to have access to the default RHEL 7 repository (refer to *Chapter 8, Yum and Repositories*, for more information), which is required for the packages that we will use.

Alternatively, you could install packages from the installation media using rpm, but you'll need to figure out the dependencies yourself.

Check the dependencies of an `rpm` using the following command:

```
~]# rpm -qpR <rpm file>
```

This will output a list of binaries, libraries, and files that you need installed prior to installing this package.

Check which package contains these files through this command:

```
~]# rpm -qlp <rpm package>
```

As you can imagine, this is a tedious job and can take quite some time as you need to figure out every dependency for every package that you want to install in this way.

Getting ready

To install a KVM, you will require at least 6 GB of free disk space, 2 GB of RAM, and an additional core or thread per guest.

Check whether your CPU supports a virtualization flag (such as SVM or VMX). Some hardware vendors disable this in the BIOS, so you may want to check your BIOS as well. Run the following command:

```
~]# grep -E 'svm|vmx' /proc/cpuinfo
flags      : ... vmx ...
```

Alternatively, you can run the following command:

```
~]# grep -E 'svm|vmx' /proc/cpuinfo
flags      : ... svm ...
```

Check whether the hardware virtualization modules (such as `kvm_intel` and `kvm`) are loaded in the kernel using the following command:

```
~]# lsmod | grep kvm
kvm_intel              155648  0
kvm                    495616  1 kvm_intel
```

How to do it...

We'll look at the three ways of installing a KVM onto your system.

Manual installation

This way of installing a KVM is generally done once the base system is installed by some other means. You need to perform the following steps:

1. Install the software needed to provide an environment to host virtualized guests with the following command:

   ```
   ~]# yum -y install qemu-kvm qemu-img libvirt
   ```

   The installation of these packages will include quite a lot of dependencies.

2. Install additional utilities required to configure libvirt and install virtual machines by running this command:

   ```
   ~]# yum -y install virt-install libvirt-python python-virthost
   libvirt-client
   ```

3. By default, the libvirt daemon is marked to autostart on each boot. Check whether it is enabled by executing the following command:

   ```
   ~]# systemctl status libvirtd

   libvirtd.service - Virtualization daemon

      Loaded: loaded (/usr/lib/systemd/system/libvirtd.service;
   enabled)

      Active: inactive

        Docs: man:libvirtd(8)

              http://libvirt.org
   ```

4. If for some reason this is not the case, mark it for autostart by executing the following:

   ```
   ~]# systemctl enable libvirtd
   ```

5. To manually stop/start/restart the libvirt daemon, this is what you'll need to execute:

   ```
   ~]# systemctl stop libvirtd
   ~]# systemctl start libvirtd
   ~]# systemctl restart libvirtd
   ```

Kickstart installation

Installing a KVM during kickstart offers you an easy way to automate the installation of KVM instances. Perform the following steps:

1. Add the following package groups to your kickstarted file in the `%packages` section:

   ```
   @virtualization-hypervisor
   @virtualization-client
   @virtualization-platform
   @virtualization-tools
   ```

2. Start the installation of your host with this kickstart file.

Graphical setup during the system's setup

This is probably the least common way of installing a KVM. The only time I used this was during the course of writing this recipe. Here's how you can do this:

1. Boot from the RHEL 7 Installation media.

2. Complete all steps besides the **Software selection** step.

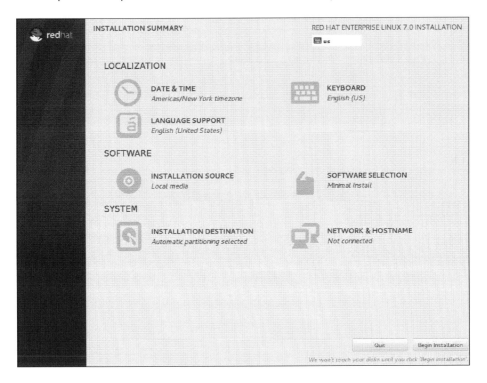

3. Go to **Software Selection** to complete the KVM software selection.

4. Select the **Virtualization host** radio button in **Base Environment,** and check the **Virtualization Platform** checkbox in **Add-Ons for Selected Environment**:

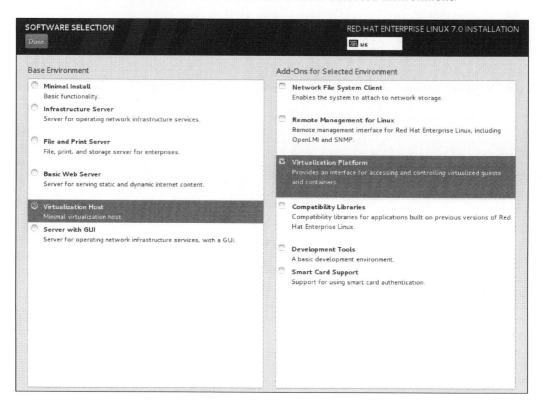

5. Finalize the installation.

6. On the **Installation Summary** screen, complete any other steps and click on **Begin Installation**.

See also

To set up your repositories, check out *Chapter 8, Yum and Repositories*.

To deploy a system using kickstart, refer to *Chapter 2, Deploying RHEL "En Masse"*.

For more in-depth information about using libvirt, go to `http://www.libvirt.org/`.

RHEL 7 has certain support limits, which are listed at these locations:

`https://access.redhat.com/articles/rhel-kvm-limits`

`https://access.redhat.com/articles/rhel-limits`

Configuring resources

Virtual machines require CPUs, memory, storage, and network access, similar to physical machines. This recipe will show you how to set up a basic KVM environment for easy resource management through libvirt.

A storage pool is a virtual container limited by two factors:

▸ The maximum size allowed by qemu-kvm

▸ The size of the disk on the physical machine

Storage pools may not exceed the size of the disk on the host. The maximum sizes are as follows:

▸ virtio-blk = 2^63 bytes or 8 exabytes (raw files or disk)

▸ EXT4 = ~ 16 TB (using 4 KB block size)

▸ XFS = ~8 exabytes

Getting ready

For this recipe, you will need a volume of at least 2 GB mounted on /vm and access to an NFS server and export.

We'll use NetworkManager to create a bridge, so ensure that you don't disable NetworkManager and have bridge-utils installed.

How to do it...

Let's have a look into managing storage pools and networks.

Creating storage pools

In order to create storage pools, we need to provide the necessary details to the KVM for it to be able to create it. You can do this as follows:

1. Create a localfs storage pool using virsh on /vm, as follows:

   ```
   ~]# virsh pool-define-as --name localfs-vm --type dir --target /vm
   ```

2. Create the target for the storage pool through the following command:

   ```
   ~# mkdir -p /nfs/vm
   ```

3. Create an NFS storage pool using `virsh` on NFS server:`/export/vm`, as follows:

```
~]# virsh pool-define-as --name nfs-vm --type network --source-
host nfsserver --source-path /export/vm –target /nfs/vm
```

4. Make the storage pools persistent across reboots through the following commands:

```
~]# virsh pool-autostart localfs-vm
```

```
~]# virsh pool-autostart nfs-vm
```

5. Start the storage pool, as follows:

```
~]# virsh pool-start localfs-vm
```

```
~]# virsh pool-start nfs-vm
```

6. Verify that the storage pools are created, started, and persistent across reboots. Run the following for this:

```
~]# virsh pool-list
  Name                             State        Autostart
  ----------------------------------------------------------
  localfs-vm                       active       yes
  nfs-vm                           active       yes
```

Querying storage pools

At some point in time, you will need to know how much space you have left in your storage pool.

Get the information of the storage pool by executing the following:

```
~]# virsh pool-info --pool <pool name>
Name:            nfs-vm
UUID:            some UUID
State:           running
Persistent:      yes
Autostart:       yes
Capacity:        499.99 GiB
Allocation:      307.33 GiB
Available:       192.66 GiB
```

As you can see, this command easily shows you its disk space allocation and availability.

Be careful though; if you use a filesystem that supports sparse files, these numbers will most likely be incorrect. You will have to manually calculate the sizes yourself!

To detect whether a file is sparse, run `ls -lhs` against the file. The `-s` command will show an additional column (the first), showing the exact space that the file is occupying, as follows:

```
~]# ls -lhs myfile
121M -rw-------. 1 root root  30G Jun 10 10:27 myfile
```

Removing storage pools

Sometimes, storage is phased out. So, it needs to be removed from the host.

You have to ensure that no guest is using volumes on the storage pool before proceeding, and you need to remove all the remaining volumes from the storage pool. Here's how to do this:

1. Remove the storage volume, as follows:

   ```
   ~]# virsh vol-delete --pool <pool name> --vol <volume name>
   ```

2. Stop the storage pool through the following command:

   ```
   ~]# virsh pool-destroy --pool <pool name>
   ```

3. Delete the storage pool using the following command:

   ```
   ~]# virsh pool-delete --pool <pool name>
   ```

Creating a virtual network

Before creating the virtual networks, we need to build a bridge over our existing network interface. For the sake of convenience, this NIC will be called `eth0`. Ensure that you record your current network configuration as we'll destroy it and recreate it on the bridge.

Unlike the storage pool, we need to create an XML configuration file to define the networks. There is no command similar to `pool-create-as` for networks. Perform the following steps:

1. Create a bridge interface on your network's interface, as follows:

   ```
   ~]# nmcli connection add type bridge autoconnect yes con-name
   bridge-eth0 ifname bridge-eth0
   ```

2. Remove your NIC's configuration using the following command:

   ```
   ~]# nmcli connection delete eth0
   ```

3. Configure your bridge, as follows:

```
~]# nmcli connection modify bridge-eth0 ipv4.addresses <ip
address/cidr> ipv4.method manual
```

```
~# nmcli connection modify bridge-eth0 ipv4.gateway <gateway ip
address>
```

```
~]# nmcli connection modify bridge-eth0 ipv4.dns <dns servers>
```

4. Finally, add your NIC to the bridge by executing the following:

```
~]# nmcli connection add type bridge-slave autoconnect yes con-
name slave-eth0 ifname eth0 master bridge-eth0
```

For starters, we'll take a look at how we can create a NATed network similar to the one that is configured by default and called the default:

1. Create the network XML configuration file, /tmp/net-nat.xml, as follows:

```
<network>
  <name>NATted</name>
  <forward mode='nat'>
    <nat>
      <port start='1024' end='65535'/>
    </nat>
  </forward>
  <bridge name='virbr0' stp='on' delay='0'/>
  <ip address='192.168.0.1' netmask='255.255.255.0'>
    <dhcp>
      <range start='192.168.0.2' end='192.168.0.254'/>
    </dhcp>
  </ip>
</network>
```

2. Define the network in the KVM using the preceding XML configuration file. Execute the following command:

```
~]# virsh net-define /tmp/net-nat.xml
```

Now, let's create a bridged network that can use the network bound to this bridge through the following steps:

1. Create the network XML configuration file, /tmp/net-bridge-eth0.xml, by running the following:

```
<network>
    <name>bridge-eth0</name>
    <forward mode="bridge" />
    <bridge name="bridge-eth0" />
</network>
```

2. Create the network in the KVM using the preceding file, as follows:

```
~]# virsh net-define /tmp/net-bridge-eth0.xml
```

There's one more type of network that is worth mentioning: the isolated network. This network is only accessible to guests defined in this network as there is no connection to the "real" world.

1. Create the network XML configuration file, `/tmp/net-local.xml`, by using the following code:

```
<network>
  <name>isolated</name>
  <bridge name='virbr1' stp='on' delay='0'/>
  <domain name='isolated'/>
</network>
```

2. Create the network in KVM by using the above file:

```
~]# virsh net-define /tmp/net-local.xml
```

Creating networks in this way will register them with the KVM but will not activate them or make them persistent through reboots. So, this is an additional step that you need to perform for each network. Now, perform the following steps:

1. Make the network persistent across reboots using the following command:

```
~]# virsh net-autostart <network name>
```

2. Activate the network, as follows:

```
~]# virsh net-start <network name>
```

3. Verify the existence of the KVM network by executing the following:

```
~]# virsh net-list --all
 Name               State       Autostart   Persistent
----------------------------------------------------------
 bridge-eth0        active      yes         yes
 default            inactive    no          yes
 isolated           active      yes         yes
 NATted             active      yes         yes
```

Removing networks

On some occasions, the networks are phased out; in this case, we need to remove the network from our setup.

Prior to executing this, you need to ensure that no guest is using the network that you want to remove. Perform the following steps to remove the networks:

1. Stop the network with the following command:

   ```
   ~# virsh net-destroy --network <network name>
   ```

2. Then, delete the network using this command:

   ```
   ~]# virsh net-undefine --network <network name>
   ```

How it works...

It's easy to create multiple storage pools using the define-pool-as command, as you can see. Every type of storage pool needs more, or fewer, arguments. In the case of the NFS storage pool, we need to specify the NFS server and export. This is done by specifying–source-host and–source-path respectively.

Creating networks is a bit more complex as it requires you to create a XML configuration file. When you want a network connected transparently to your physical networks, you can only use bridged networks as it is impossible to bind a network straight to your network's interface.

There's more...

The storage backend created in this recipe is not the limit. Libvirt also supports the following backend pools:

Local storage pools

Local storage pools are directly connected to the physical machine. They include local directories, disks, partitions, and LVM volume groups. Local storage pools are not suitable for enterprises as these do not support live migration.

Networked or shared storage pools

Network storage pools include storage shared through standard protocols over a network. This is required when we migrate virtual machines between physical hosts. The supported network storage protocols are Fibre Channel-based LUNs, iSCSI, NFS, GFS2, and SCSI RDMA.

By defining the storage pools and networks in libvirt, you ensure the availability of the resources for your guest. If, for some reason, the resource is unavailable, the KVM will not attempt to start the guests that use these resources.

When checking out the man page for *virsh (1)*, you will find a similar command to `net-define`, `pool-define`: `net-create`, and `pool-create` (and `pool-create-as`). The `net-create` command, similar to `pool-create` and `pool-create-as`, creates transient (or temporary) resources, which will be gone when libvirt is restarted. On the other hand, `net-define` and `pool-define` (as also `pool-define-as`) create persistent (or permanent) resources, which will still be there after you restart libvirt.

See also

You can find out more on libvirt storage backend pools at `https://libvirt.org/storage.html`

More information on libvirt networking can be found at `http://wiki.libvirt.org/page/Networking`

Building guests

After you install and configure a KVM on the host system, you can create guest operating systems. Every guest is defined by a set of resources and parameters stored in the XML format. When you want to create a new guest, creating such an XML file is quite cumbersome. There are two ways to create a guest:

- ▶ Using `virt-manager`
- ▶ Using `virt-install`

This recipe will employ the latter as it is perfect for scripting, while `virt-manager` is a GUI and not very well suited to automate things.

Getting ready

In this recipe, we will cover a generic approach to create a new virtual machine using the `bridge-eth0` network bridge and create a virtual disk on the `localfs-vm` storage pool, which is formatted as QCOW2. The QCOW2 format is a popular virtual disk format as it allows thin provisioning and snapshotting. We will boot the RHEL 7 installation media located on the `localfs-iso` storage pool (`rhel7-install.iso`) to start installing a new RHEL 7 system.

How to do it...

Let's create some guests and delete them.

Create a guest

Let's first create a disk for the guest and then create the guest on this disk, as follows:

1. Create a 10 GB QCOW2 format disk in the `localfs-vm` pool, as follows:

   ```
   ~]# virsh vol-create-as --pool localfs-vm --name rhel7_guest-vda.qcows2 --format qcows2 –capacity 10G
   ```

2. Create the virtual machine and start it through the following command:

   ```
   ~]# virt-install \
   --hvm \
   --name rhel7_guest \
   --memory=2048,maxmemory=4096 \
   --vcpus=2,maxvcpus=4 \
   --os-type linux \
   --os-variant rhel7 \
   --boot hd,cdrom,network,menu=on \
   --controller type=scsi,model=virtio-scsi \
   --disk device=cdrom,vol=localfs-iso/rhel7-install.iso,readonly=on,bus=scsi \
   --disk device=disk,vol=localfs-vm/rhel7_guest-vda.qcow2,cache=none,bus=scsi \
   --network network=bridge-eth0,model=virtio \
   --graphics vnc \
   --graphics spice \
   --noautoconsole \
   --memballoon virtio
   ```

Deleting a guest

At some point, you'll need to remove the guests. You can do this as follows:

1. First, ensure that the guest is down by running the following:

   ```
   ~]# virsh list –all
    Id    Name                         State
   ------------------------------------------------------
    -      rhel7_guest                  shut off
   ```

   If the state is not `shut off`, you can forcefully shut it down:

   ```
   ~]# virsh destroy --domain <guest name>
   ```

2. List the storage volumes in use by your guest and copy this somewhere:

```
~]# virsh domblklist <guest name>

Type        Device      Target      Source
--------------------------------------------------
file        disk        vda         /vm/rhel7_guest-vda.qcow2
file        cdrom       hda         /iso/rhel7-install.iso
```

3. Delete the guest through the following command:

```
~]# virsh undefine --domain <guest name> --storage vda
```

Adding `--remove-all-storage` to the command will wipe off the data on the storage volumes dedicated to this guest prior to deleting the volume from the pool.

How it works...

The `virt-install` command supports creating storage volumes (disks) by specifying the pool, size, and format. However, if this storage volume already exists, the application will fail. Depending on the speed of your KVM host disks (local or network) and the size of the guest's disks, the process of creating a new disk may take some time to be completed. By specifying an existing disk with `virt-install`, you can reuse the disk should you need to reinstall the guest. It would be possible to only create the disk on the first pass and change your command line appropriately after this. However, the fact remains that using `virsh vol-create-as` gives you more granular control of what you want to do.

We're using the QCOW2 format to contain the guest's disk as it is a popular format when it comes to storing KVM guest disks. This is because it supports thin provisioning and snapshotting.

When creating the guest, we specify both the `maxmemory` option for memory configuration and the `maxvcpus` option for vcpus configuration. This will allow us to add CPUs and RAM to the guest while it is running. If we do not assign these, we'll have to shut down the system before being able to change the XML configuration using the following command:

```
~# virsh edit <hostname>
```

As you can see, we're using the `virtio` driver for any hardware (network, disks, or balloon) that supports it as it is native to the KVM and is included in the RHEL 7 kernel.

> If, for some reason, your guest OS doesn't support `virtio` drivers, you should remove the `--controller` option of the command line and the bus specification from the `--disk` option.
>
> For more information on `virtio` support, go to `http://wiki.libvirt.org/page/Virtio`.

The `--memballoon` option will ensure that we do not run into problems when we overcommit our memory. When specific guests require more memory, the ballooning driver will ensure that the "idle" guests' memory can be evenly redistributed.

The `graphics` option will allow you to connect to the guest through the host using either VNC (which is a popular client to control remote computers) or spice (which is the default client for `virt-manager`). The configuration for both VNC and spice is insecure, though. You can either set this up by specifying a password—by adding `password=<password>` to each graphics stanza—or by editing the `/etc/libvirt/qemu.conf` file on the KVM host, which will be applied to all guests.

There's more...

In this recipe, we used "local" install media in the form of an ISO image to install the system. However, it is also possible to install a guest without a CD, DVD, or an ISO image. The `--location` installation method option allows you to specify a URI that contains your kernel/ initrd pair, which is required to start the installation.

Using `--location` in combination with `--extra-args` will allow you to specify kernel command-line arguments to pass to the installer. This can be used, for instance, to pass on the location of an Anaconda kickstart file for automated installs and/or specifying your IP configuration during the installer.

See also

Check the man page of *virt-install (1)* for more information on how to use it to your advantage.

Adding CPUs on the fly

Imagine an enterprise having to correctly add dimension to all their systems right from the start. In my experience, this is very difficult. You will either underdimension it, and your customers will complain about performance at some point, or you will overdimension it, and then the machine will sit there, idling about, which is not optimal either. This is the reason hardware vendors have come up with `hot-add` resources. This allows a system to have its CPUs, memory, and/or disks to be upgraded/increased without the need for a shutdown. A KVM implements a similar functionality for its guests. It allows you to increase the CPUs, memory, and disks on the fly.

The actual recipe is very simple to execute, but there are some prerequisites to be met.

Getting ready

In order to be able to add CPUs on the fly to a guest, the guest's configuration must support them.

There are two ways to achieve this:

- ▶ It must be created with the max option, as follows:

  ```
  --vcpus 2,maxvcpus=4
  ```

- ▶ You can set the maximum using `virsh` (which will be applied at the next boot) through the following command:

  ```
  ~]# virsh setvcpus --domain <guestname> --count <max cpu count>
  --config --maximum
  ```

- ▶ You can edit the guests' XML files, as follows:

  ```
  ~]# virsh edit <guestname>
  ```

The last two options will require you to shut down and boot (not reboot) your guest as these commands cannot change the "live" configuration.

The guest's XML file must contain the following element with the subsequent attributes:

```
<domain type='kvm'>
...
<vcpu current='2'>4</vcpu>
...
</domain>
```

Here, `current` indicates the number of CPUs in use, and the number within the node indicates the maximum number of vCPUs that can be assigned. This number can be increased but should never exceed the number of cores or threads in your host.

How to do it...

Let's add some CPUs to the guest.

On the KVM host, perform the following steps:

1. Get the maximum number vCPUs that you can assign, as follows:

   ```
   ~]# virsh dumpxml <guestname> |grep vcpu
   <vcpu placement='static' current='4'>8</vcpu>
   ```

2. Now, set the new number of vCPUs through this command:

```
~]# virsh setvcpus --domain <guestname> --count <# of CPUs> --live
```

On the KVM guest, perform the following:

1. Tell your guest OS there are more CPUs available by executing the following command:

```
~]# for i in $(grep -H 0 /sys/devices/system/cpu/cpu*/online | awk
-F: '{print $1}'); do echo 1 > $i; done
```

Adding RAM on the fly

As with CPUs, the possibility to add memory on the fly is an added value in mission-critical environments where downtime can literally cost a company millions of Euros.

The recipe presented here is quite simple, similar to the one on CPUs. Here, your guest needs to be prepared to use this functionality as well.

Getting ready

If you want to be able to add memory on the fly to a guest, it must be configured to support it. As with the CPU, this has to be activated. There are three ways to do this:

▶ The guest must be created with the maxmem option, as follows:

```
--memory 2G,maxmemory=4G
```

▶ You can set the maximum memory using the virsh command, as follows:

```
~]# virsh setmaxmem --domain <guestname> --size <max mem> --live
```

▶ You can edit the guests' XML files:

```
~]# virsh edit <guestname>
```

Of course, the latter 2 option requires you to shut down the guest, which is not always possible in production environments.

Ensure that the guests' XML configuration files contain the following elements with the subsequent attributes:

```
<domain type='kvm'>
...
    <memory unit='KiB'>4194304</memory>
    <currentMemory unit='KiB'>2097152</currentMemory>
...
</domain>
```

How to do it...

Let's increase the guest's memory.

On the KVM host, perform the following steps:

1. Get the current and maximum memory allocation for a guest, as follows:

    ```
    ~]# virsh dumpxml srv00002 |grep -i memory
      <memory unit='KiB'>4194304</memory>
      <currentMemory unit='KiB'>4194304</currentMemory>
    ```

2. Set the new amount of memory for the guest by executing the following command:

    ```
    ~]# virsh setmem --domain <guestname> --size <memory> --live
    ```

On the KVM guest, perform the following:

1. Tell your guest OS about the memory increase through this command:

    ```
    ~]# for i in $(grep -H offline /sys/devices/system/memory/memory*/
    state | awk -F: '{print $1}'); do echo online > $i; done
    ```

Adding disks on the fly

This recipe includes instructions on how to create different types of storage volumes. Storage volumes are dedicated storage sets aside for use by guests.

Getting ready

There is not a lot of preparation to be done in order to add disks to your guest, which is in contrast to adding CPUs and RAM.

You only need to ensure that the storage pool has enough free disk space to accommodate the new disk.

How to do it...

Similar to the recipe for creating guests, you'll need to create a disk first. This can be done as follows:

1. Let's create a raw disk in the `localfs-vm` pool that is `30` GB big through the following command:

    ```
    ~]# virsh vol-create-as --pool localfs-vm --name rhel7_guest-vdb.
    raw --format raw --capacity 30G
    ```

2. Look up the path of the newly created volume, as follows:

    ```
    ~]# virsh vol-list --pool localfs-vm |awk '$1 ~ /^rhel7_guest-vdb.
    raw$/ {print $2}'
    ```

    This will result in the path of your volume; here's an example:

    ```
    /vm/rhel7_guest-vdb.raw
    ```

3. Attach the disk to the guest, as follows:

    ```
    ~]# virsh attach-disk --domain <guestname> --source <the above
    path> --target vdb --cache none --persistent -live
    ```

How it works...

Creating a disk using `vol-create-as` may take some time depending on the speed of your host's disks and the size of the guest's disks.

We will look up the path of the newly created volume as it is a required argument for the command that attaches the disk to the guest. In most cases, you won't need to do this as you'll know how your host is configured, but when you script this kind of functionality, you will require this step.

Adding a disk in this way will attach a disk using the `virtio` driver, which, as specified earlier, is optimized for use with KVMs.

There's more...

If, for some reason, the original guest doesn't support `virtio` drivers or you do not have the `virtio` controller, you can create this yourself. Store the XML configuration file as `/tmp/controller.xml` with the following contents:

```
<controller type='scsi' model='virtio' />
```

You can find this out by checking the host's XML file for the preceding statement.

Then, import the XML configuration file, as follows:

```
~]# virsh attach-device –domain <guestname> /tmp/controller.xml
```

This will allow you to create disks using `virtio`.

Moving disks to another storage

Moving disks around is part of the life cycle of a guest. Disks in the storage pools (local or network) may fail or fill up due to bad capacity management. Another reason may be the cost or speed of the disks involved. Sooner or later, one of these things will happen, and then you will need to move the storage somewhere else.

Ordinarily, one would have to shut down the guest, copy the storage volume file elsewhere (if it is a file), wait, update the machine's XML configuration, and launch it again. However, in today's mission-critical enterprises, this may not always be possible.

Getting ready

In order to perform this copy, you need the source and destination paths of the disk. You can get the source path by checking the XML configuration file or, even better, by querying the storage volume itself. This does require you to know which storage pool it is located on.

Execute the following command:

```
~]# virsh vol-list --pool <storage pool> |awk '$1 ~ /^<volume name>$/
{print $2}'
```

Ensure that your destination is an existing storage pool; if not, go ahead and create it.

Check out the *Configuring resources* recipe in this chapter to create storage pools.

If you can't remember the path to your pool's location, run the following:

```
~]# virsh pool-dumpxml <poolname> |awk '/<path>.*<\/path>/ {print $1}'
```

How to do it...

Moving disks can take some time, so ensure that you have plenty of time available. Perform the following steps:

1. Dump the inactive XML configuration file for the guest, as follows:

   ```
   ~]# virsh dumpxml --inactive <guestname> > /tmp/<guestname>.xml
   ```

   The `--inactive` file will ensure that it doesn't copy any temporary information that is irrelevant to the guest.

2. Undefine the guest through the following command:

   ```
   ~]# virsh undefine <guestname>
   ```

3. Copy the virtual disk to another location by executing the following:

   ```
   ~]# virsh blockcopy --domain <guestname> --path <original path>
   --dest <destination path> --wait --verbose --pivot
   ```

4. Now, edit the guest's XML configuration file and change the path of the disk to the new location.

5. Redefine the guest, as follows:

   ```
   ~]# virsh define /tmp/<guestname>.xml
   ```

6. Remove the source disk after you are happy with the results. Run the following command:

   ```
   ~]# virsh vol-delete --pool <poolname> --vol <volname>
   ```

How it works...

The moving of disks can only be performed on transient domains, which is the reason we execute the `virsh undefine` command. In order to be able to make it persistent again after the transfer, we also need to dump the XML configuration file and modify the storage volume path.

Moving the disk does two things, which are:

▶ Firstly, it copies all the data of the source to the destination

▶ Secondly, when the copying is complete, both source and destination remain mirrored until it is either canceled with `blockjob --abort` or actually switched over to the new target by executing the `blockjob --pivot` command

The preceding `blockcopy` command does everything at the same time. The `--wait` command will not give control back to the user until the command fails or succeeds. It is essentially the same as the following:

```
~]# virsh blockcopy --domain <guestname> --path <source path> --dest
<destination path>
```

Monitor the progress of the copy by executing the following:

```
~]# watch -n10 "virsh blockjob –domain <guestname> --path <source path>
--info"
```

When it's done, execute this:

```
~]# virsh blockjob –domain <guestname> --path <source path> --pivot
```

There's more...

It is also possible to change the disk format on the fly, by specifying the `--format` argument with the format that you want to convert your disk into. If you want to copy it to a block device, specify `--blockdev`.

Moving VMs

Moving disks will mitigate the risk of failing disks. When your CPUs, memory, and other non-disk-related components start failing, you have no other option but to move the guests to other host(s).

The recipe for this task is rather simple, but it's the prerequisites that can make it succeed or fail miserably.

Getting ready

The prerequisites for this recipe are quite extended.

For the host, the following are the requirements:

- You'll need to have access to shared data. Both the source and destination KVM machine will need to be able to access the same storage—for example, iSCSI, NFS, and so on.
- Both hosts need the same type of CPU—that is, Intel or AMD (one cannot live migrate a guest from a host with Intel CPUs to a host with AMD CPUs).
- Both hosts need to be installed with the same version and updates of libvirt.
- Both hosts need to have the same network ports open.
- Both hosts must have identical KVM network configurations or at least the same network configurations for the interfaces used by the guest.
- Both hosts must be accessible through the network.
- It's a good idea to have a management network set up and connected to the two hosts, which can be used for data transfer. This will cause less network traffic on your "production" network and increase the overall speed.
- The `No execution` bit must be the same on both hosts.

The requirement for the guest is:

- The `cache=none` must be specified for all block devices that are opened in write mode.

How to do it...

There are multiple ways to migrate hosts, but we will only highlight the two most common ways.

Live native migration over the default network

This process to migrate a host is luckily very simple and can be summarized in one command.

On the source host, execute the following:

```
~]# virsh migrate --domain <guestname> --live --persistent
--undefinesource --verbose --desturl qemu+ssh://<host 2>/system
```

Live native migration over a dedicated network

It is possible to perform the migration over a dedicated network. By default, this will use the first network it finds that suits it needs. You'll need to specify the listening address (on the host) and the protocol. This requires the same command as before, but we'll need to specify the local listening IP address and protocol, such as TCP.

On the source host, execute the following:

```
~]# virsh migrate --domain <guestname> --live --persistent
--undefinesource --verbose --desturl qemu+ssh://<host 2>/system
tcp://<local ip address on dedicated network>/
```

How it works...

This type of migration is called a "hypervisor native" transport. The biggest advantage of this type of migration is that it incurs the lowest computational cost by minimizing the number of data copies involved.

When we migrate a host, it performs a copy of the memory of the guest to the new host. When the copying is successful, it kills the guest on the source host and starts it on the new host. As the memory is copied, the interruption will be very short-lived.

There's more...

Communication between the two hosts is over SSH, which is already pretty secure. However, it's also possible to tunnel the data over an even more strongly encrypted channel by specifying the --tunnelled option. This will impose more traffic on your network as there will be extra data communication between the two hosts.

The --compress option can help you out if you wish to reduce the traffic over your network, but this will increase the load on both your hosts as they need to compress/decompress the data, which, in turn, may impact your guests performance. If time is not of the essence but traffic is, this is a good solution.

There's very good and in-depth documentation about this process at `https://libvirt.org/migration.html`.

Backing up your VM metadata

While a KVM stores some of the resources' configuration on the disk in a human readable format, it is a good idea to query libvirt for the configuration of your resources.

How to do it...

In this recipe we'll back up all relevant KVM metadata by performing the following steps:

Here's the network configuration:

```
~]# for i in $(virsh net-list --all | sed -e '1,2d' |awk '{print $1}');
do \
    virsh net-dumpxml --network $i --inactive > /tmp/net-$i.xml; \
done
```

Here's the storage configuration:

```
~]# for i in $(virsh pool-list --all | sed -e '1,2d' |awk '{print $1}');
do \
    for j in $(virsh vol-list --pool $i |sed -e '1,2d') | awk '{print
$1}'; do \
        virsh vol-dumpxml --pool $i --vol $j > /tmp/vol-$j.xml; \
    done \
    virsh pool-dumpxml --pool $i --inactive > /tmp/pool-$i.xml; \
done
```

Here's the guest configuration:

```
~]# for i in $(virsh list --all | sed -e '1,2d' |awk '{print $1}'); do \
    virsh dumpxml --domain $i --inactive > /tmp/domain-$i.xml; \
done
```

How it works...

The `virsh net-dumpxml` command allows you to dump the precise configuration of the specified network. In combination with `virsh net-list`, you can create a loop that enumerates all networks and dumps them on the file. By specifying `--all`, you will export all networks, even those that are not active. If you do not wish to back up the configuration for nonactive networks, substitute `virsh net-list --all` with `virsh net-list`.

Storage pools can be enumerated, similarly to networks, using `virsh net-list`. However, besides the individual storage pool configuration, we are also interested in the configuration of individual storage volumes. Luckily, both implement a `list` and `dumpxml` command! If you're not interested in nonactive pools, you can omit the `--all` option with `virsh pool-list`.

Guests can similarly be enumerated and their XML configuration dumped using `dumpxml`. Again, if you're not interested in nonactive guests, you can omit the `--all` option with `virsh list`.

See also

The man page for *virsh (1)* lists all the possible options for the commands used in the preceding section.

2

Deploying RHEL "En Masse"

In this chapter, the following recipes are provided:

- ▶ Creating a kickstart file
- ▶ Publishing your kickstart file using `httpd`
- ▶ Deploying a system using `pxe`
- ▶ Deploying a system using a custom boot ISO file

Introduction

In this chapter, you will find the answer to deploying multiple systems with the same basic setup. We will first look at creating an answer file, the kickstart file that will drive the unattended installation. Then, we'll take a look at a possible way to make this kickstart file accessible through the Apache web server. Finally, we'll discuss two common ways to install physical and virtual machines.

This chapter assumes that you have a working knowledge of system network configuration components, such as DNS, DNS search, IP addresses, and so on, and yum repositories.

Creating a kickstart file

A kickstart file is essentially a file containing all the necessary answers to questions that are asked during a typical install. It was created by Red Hat in response to the need for automated installs. Using kickstart, an admin can create one file or template containing all the instructions.

There are three ways to create a kickstart file:

- ▸ By hand
- ▸ Using the GUI's `system-config-kickstart` tool
- ▸ Using the standard Red Hat installation program Anaconda

In this recipe, I will cover a combination of the first two.

Getting ready

Before we can get down to the nitty-gritty of generating our base kickstart file or template, we need to install `system-config-kickstart`. Run the following command:

```
~# yum install -y system-config-kickstart
```

How to do it...

First, let's create a base template for our kickstart file(s) through the following steps:

1. First, launch **Kickstart Configurator** from the menu.

2. Select your system's basic configuration from the **Kickstart Configurator** GUI.

   The following screenshot shows the options you can set in the **Basic Configuration** view:

3. Now, select the installation method from the **Kickstart Configurator** GUI.

The following screenshot shows the options that you can set in the **Installation method** view:

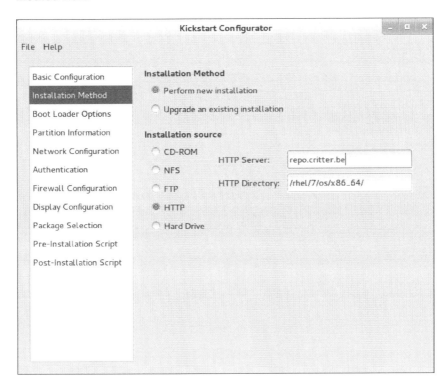

4. Next, substitute the values for **HTTP Server** and **HTTP Directory** with your own repositories.

5. Ensure that the correct settings are applied for **Boot Loader**.

The following screenshot shows the options that you can set in the **Boot Loader options** view:

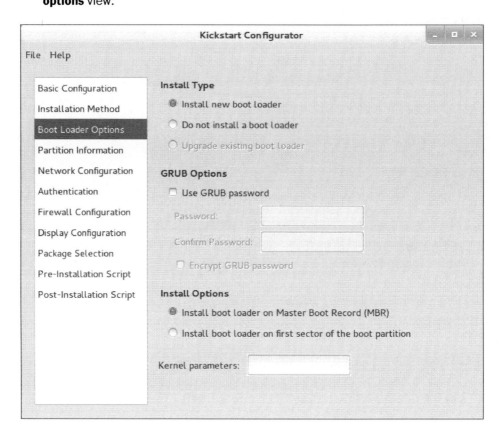

6. Configure your disk and partition information. Simply create a `/boot` partition and be done with it! We'll edit the file manually for better customization.

   The following screenshot shows the options you can set in the **Partition Information** view:

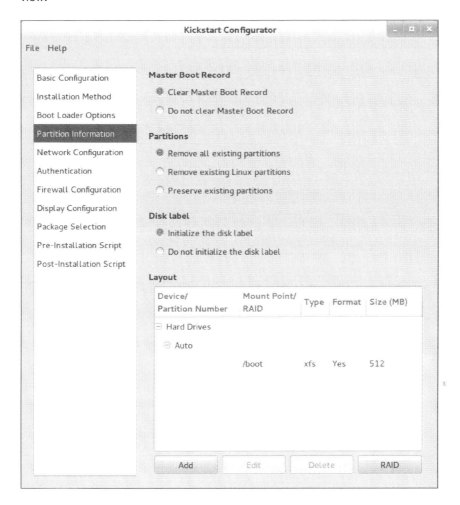

7. Configure your network. You need to know the name of your device if you want to correctly configure your network.

The following screenshot shows the **Network Device** information that you can edit in the **Network Configuration** view:

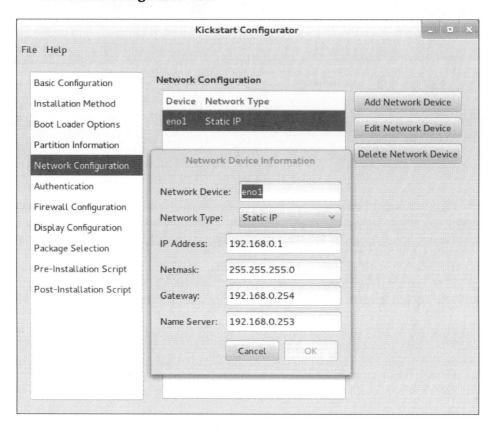

8. Now, disable **Installing a graphical environment**.

    We want as few packages as possible. The following screenshot shows the options that you can set in the **Display Configuration** view:

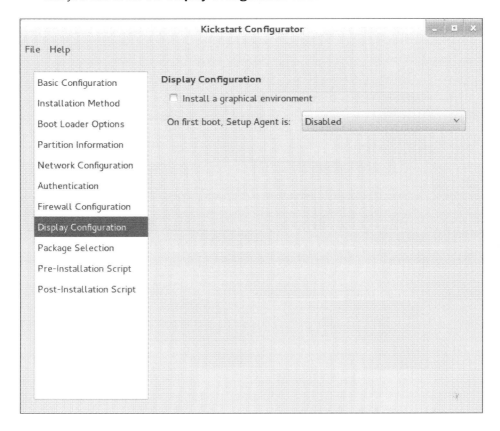

9. Next, perform any preinstallation and/or postinstallation tasks you deem necessary. I always try to make root accessible through SSH and keys.

   The following screenshot shows the options that you can set in the **Post-Installation Script** view:

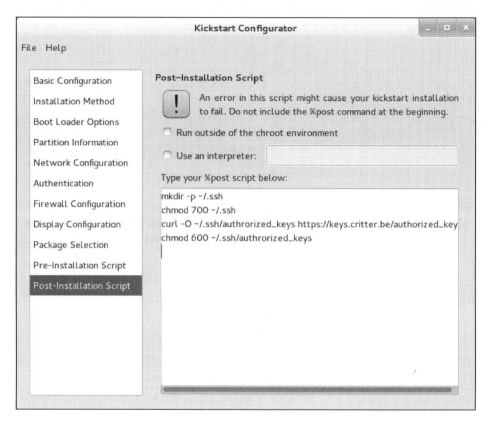

10. Save the kickstart file.

11. Open the file using your favorite editor and add the following to your partition section:

```
part pv.01 --size=1 --ondisk=sda --grow
volgroup vg1 pv.01
logvol / --vgname=vg1 --size=2048 --name=root
logvol /usr --vgname=vg1 --size=2048 --name=usr
logvol /var --vgname=vg1 --size=2048 --name=var
logvol /var/log --vgname=vg1 --size=1024 --name=var
logvol /home --vgname=vg1 --size=512 --name=home
logvol swap --vgname=vg1 --recommended --name=swap –fstype=swap
```

12. Now, add the following script to your network line:

```
--hostname=rhel7
```

13. Add the following script before `%post`:

```
%packages -nobase
@core --nodefaults
%end
```

14. Create a password hash for use in the next step, as follows:

~]# openssl passwd -1 "MySuperSecretRootPassword"

1mecIlXKN$6VRdaRkevjw9nngcMtRlO.

15. Save the resulting file. You should have something similar to this:

```
#platform=x86, AMD64, or Intel EM64T
#version=DEVEL
# Install OS instead of upgrade
install
# Keyboard layouts
keyboard 'be-latin1'
# Halt after installation
halt
# Root password
rootpw --iscrypted $1$mecIlXKN$6VRdaRkevjw9nngcMtRlO.
# System timezone
timezone Europe/Brussels
# Use network installation
url --url="http://repo.example.com/rhel/7/os/x86_64/"
# System language
lang en_US
# Firewall configuration
firewall --disabled
# Network information
network  --bootproto=static --device=eno1 --
gateway=192.168.0.254 --ip=192.168.0.1 --nameserver=192.168.0.253
--netmask=255.255.255.0 --hostname=rhel7
# System authorization information
auth  --useshadow  --passalgo=sha512
# Use text mode install
text
# SELinux configuration
selinux --enforcing
# Do not configure the X Window System
skipx
```

```
# System bootloader configuration
bootloader --location=none
# Clear the Master Boot Record
zerombr
# Partition clearing information
clearpart --all --initlabel
# Disk partitioning information
part /boot --fstype="xfs" --ondisk=sda --size=512
part pv.01 --size=1 --ondisk=sda --grow
volgroup vg1 pv.01
logvol / --vgname=vg1 --size=2048 --name=root --fstype=xfs
logvol /usr --vgname=vg1 --size=2048 --name=usr --fstype=xfs
logvol /var --vgname=vg1 --size=2048 --name=var --fstype=xfs
logvol /var/log --vgname=vg1 --size=1024 --name=var --fstype=xfs
logvol /home --vgname=vg1 --size=512 --name=home --fstype=xfs
logvol swap --vgname=vg1 --recommended --name=swap --fstype=swap

%packages --nobase
@core --nodefaults
%end

%post
mkdir -p ~/.ssh
chmod 700 ~/.ssh
# Let's download my authorized keyfile from my key
server...
curl -O ~/.ssh/authrorized_keys
https://keys.example.com/authorized_keys
chmod 600 ~/.ssh/authrorized_keys
%end
```

How it works...

The `system-config-kickstart` is used to generate a minimal install as any addition would be more complex than the tool can handle and we need to be able to add them manually/dynamically afterwards. The fewer the number of packages the better as you'll need to apply bug and security fixes for every package installed.

Although the GUI allows us to configure the brunt of the options we need, I prefer tweaking some portions of them manually as they are not as straightforward through the GUI.

Step 9 adds the necessary information to use the rest of the disk as an LVM physical volume and partitions it so that *big* filesystems can easily be extended if necessary.

The `--recommended` argument for the SWAP partition creates a swap partition as per the swap size recommendations set by Red Hat.

Step 10 adds a hostname for your host. If you do not specify this, the system will attempt to resolve the IP address and use this hostname. If it cannot determine any hostname, it will use `localhost.localdomain` as `fqdn`.

Step 11 ensures that only the core system is installed and nothing more, so you can build from here.

If you want to know exactly which packages are installed in the core group, run the following command on an RHEL 7 system:

```
~# yum groupinfo core
```

There's more...

I didn't cover one option that I mentioned in the *Getting Ready* section as it is automatically generated when you install a system manually. The file can be found after installation at `/root/anaconda-ks.cfg`. Instead of using the `system-config-kickstart` tool to generate a kickstart file, you can use this file to get started.

Starting with RHEL 7, kickstart deployments support add-ons. These add-ons can expand the standard kickstart installation in many ways. To use kickstart add-ons, just add the `%addon addon_name` option followed by `%end`, as with the `%pre` and `%post` sections. Anaconda comes with the `kdump` add-on, which you can use to install and configure `kdump` during the installation by providing the following section in your kickstart file:

```
%addon com_redhat_kdump --enable --reserve-mb=auto
%end
```

See also

For more detailed information about kickstart files, refer to the website `https://github.com/rhinstaller/pykickstart/blob/master/docs/kickstart-docs.rst`.

For the consistent network device naming, refer to `https://access.redhat.com/documentation/en-US/Red_Hat_Enterprise_Linux/7/html/Networking_Guide/ch-Consistent_Network_Device_Naming.html`.

Publishing your kickstart file using httpd

You can save your kickstart file to a USB stick (or any other medium), but this becomes a bit cumbersome if you need to install multiple systems in different locations.

Loading kickstart files over the network from the kernel line during an install only supports NFS, HTTP, and FTP.

In this recipe, I choose HTTP as it is a common technology within companies and easy to secure.

How to do it...

Let's start by installing Apache `httpd`, as follows:

1. Install Apache `httpd` through the following command:

   ```
   ~]# yum install -y httpd
   ```

2. Enable and start the `httpd` daemon, as follows:

   ```
   ~]# systemctl enable httpd
   ln -s '/usr/lib/systemd/system/httpd.service' '/etc/systemd/
   system/multi-user.target.wants/httpd.service'
   ~]# systemctl start httpd
   ```

3. Create a directory to contain the kickstart file(s) by running the following command:

   ```
   ~]# mkdir -p /var/www/html/kickstart
   ~]# chown apache:apache /var/www/html/kickstart
   ~]# chmod 750 /var/www/html/kickstart
   ```

4. Copy your kickstart file to this new location:

   ```
   ~]# cp kickstart.ks /var/www/html/kickstart/
   ```

5. In a browser, browse to the kickstart directory on your web server, as shown in the following screenshot:

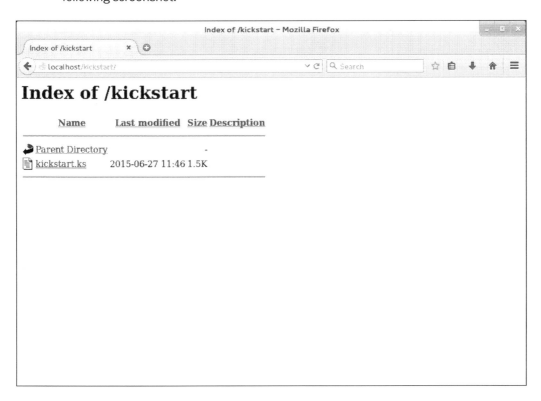

There's more...

In this way, you can create multiple kickstart files, which will be available from anywhere in your network.

Additionally, you could use CGI-BIN, PHP, or any other technology that has an Apache module to dynamically create kickstart files based on the arguments that you specify in the URL.

An alternative to creating your own solution for dynamic kickstart files is Cobbler.

See also

For more info on Cobbler, go to `http://cobbler.github.io/`.

Deploying a system using PXE

PXE, or Preboot eXecution Environment, allows you to instruct computers to boot using network resources. This allows you to control a single source to install servers without the need to physically insert cumbersome DVDs or USB sticks.

Getting ready

For this recipe, you will need a fully working RHEL 7 repository.

How to do it...

With this recipe, we'll install and configure PXE boots from the RHEL 7 installation media, as follows:

1. Install the necessary packages using the following command:

   ```
   ~]# yum install -y dnsmasq syslinux tftp-server
   ```

2. Configure the DNSMASQ server by editing /etc/dnsmasq.conf, as follows:

   ```
   # interfaces to bind to
   interface=eno1,lo
   # the domain for this DNS server
   domain=rhel7.lan
   # DHCP lease range
   dhcp-range= eno1,192.168.0.3,192.168.0.103,255.255.255.0,1h
   # PXE - the address of the PXE server
   dhcp-boot=pxelinux.0,pxeserver,192.168.0.1
   # Gateway
   dhcp-option=3,192.168.0.254
   # DNS servers for DHCP clients(your internal DNS servers,
   and one of Google's DNS servers)
   dhcp-option=6,192.168.1.1, 8.8.8.8
   # DNS server to forward DNS queries to
   server=8.8.4.4
   # Broadcast Address
   dhcp-option=28,192.168.0.255
   pxe-prompt="Press F1 for menu.", 60
   pxe-service=x86_64PC, "Install RHEL 7 from network",
   pxelinux
   enable-tftp
   tftp-root=/var/lib/tftpboot
   ```

3. Enable and start `dnsmasq` using the following:

   ```
   ~]# systemctl enable dnsmasq
   ~]# systemctl start dnsmasq
   ```

4. Now, enable and start the `xinet` daemon by running the following:

   ```
   ~]# systemctl enable xinetd
   ~]# systemctl start xinetd
   ```

5. Enable the `tftp` server's `xinet` daemon, as follows:

   ```
   ~]# sed -i '/disable/ s/yes/no/' /etc/xinetd.d/tftp
   ```

6. Copy the `syslinux` boot loaders to the `tftp` server's boot directory by executing the following command:

   ```
   ~]# cp -r /usr/share/syslinux/* /var/lib/tftpboot
   ```

7. Next, create the PXE configuration directory using this command:

   ```
   ~]# mkdir /var/lib/tftpboot/pxelinux.cfg
   ```

8. Then, create the PXE configuration file, as follows: `/var/lib/tftpboot/pxelinux.cfg/default`.

   ```
   default menu.c32
   prompt 0
   timeout 300
   ONTIMEOUT local
   menu title PXE Boot Menu
   label 1
      menu label ^1 - Install RHEL 7 x64 with Local http Repo
      kernel rhel7/vmlinuz
      append initrd=rhel7/initrd.img method=http://repo.critter.be/
   rhel/7/os/x86_64/
   devfs=nomount ks=http://kickstart.critter.be/kickstart.ks
   label 2
      menu label ^2 - Boot from local media
   ```

9. Copy `initrd` and `kernel` from the RHEL 7 installation media to `/var/lib/tftpboot/rhel7/`, and run the following commands:

   ```
   ~]# mkdir /var/lib/tftpboot/rhel7
   ~]# mount -o loop /dev/cdrom /mnt
   ~]# cp /mnt/images/pxeboot/{initrd.img,vmlinuz} /var/lib/tftpboot/
   rhel7/
   ~]# umount /mnt
   ```

10. Open the firewall on your server using these commands (however, this may not be necessary):

```
~]# firewall-cmd --add-service=dns --permanent
~]# firewall-cmd --add-service=dhcp --permanent
~]# firewall-cmd --add-service=tftp --permanent
~]# firewall-cmd --reload
```

11. Finally, launch your client, configure it to boot from the network, and select the first option shown in the following figure:

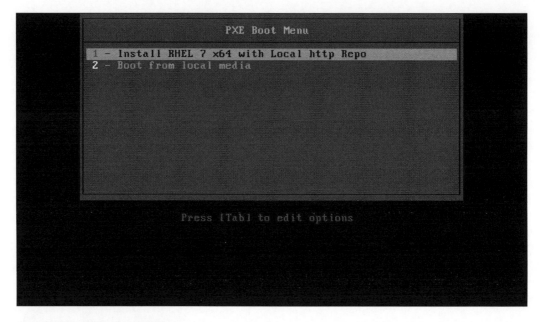

How it works...

DNSMASQ takes care of pointing booting systems to the `tftp` server by providing the `enable-tftp` option in the `dnsmasq` configuration file.

Syslinux is needed to provide the necessary binaries to boot from the network.

The `tftp` server itself provides access to the `syslinux` files, RHEL 7 kernel, and `initrd` for the system to boot from.

The PXE configuration file provides the necessary configuration to boot a system, including a kickstart file that automatically installs your system.

There's more...

This recipe's base premise is that you do not have a DHCP server installed. In most companies, you already have DHCP services available.

If you have an ISC-DHCP server in place, this is what you need to add to the subnet definition(s) you want to allow in PXE:

```
next-server <ip address of TFTP server>;
filename "pxelinux.0";
```

See also

Check out *Chapter 8, Yum and Repositories* to set up an RHEL 7 repository from the installation media.

Deploying a system using a custom boot ISO file

PXE is a widely used way to deploy systems, and so are ISO's. PXE may not always be at hand because of security, hardware availability, and so on.

Many hardware manufacturers provide remote access to their systems without an OS installed. HP has iLO, while Dell has RIB. The advantage of these "remote" control solutions is that they also allow you to mount "virtual" media in the form of an ISO.

How to do it...

Red Hat provides boot media as ISO images, which you can use to boot your systems from. We will create a custom ISO image, which will allow us to boot a system in a similar way.

Let's create an ISO that you can mount as virtual media, write a CD-ROM, or even use dd to write the contents on a USB stick/disk through the following steps:

1. Install the required packages to create ISO9660 images, as follows:

   ```
   ~]# yum install -y genisoimage
   ```

2. Mount the RHEL 7 DVD's ISO image by executing the following command:

   ```
   ~]# mount -o loop /path/to/rhel-server-7.0-x86_64-dvd.iso /mnt
   ```

3. Copy the required files for the custom ISO from the RHEL 7 media via the following commands:

    ```
    ~]# mkdir -p /root/iso
    ~]# cp -r /mnt/isolinux /root/iso
    ~]# umount /mnt
    ```

4. Now, unmount the RHEL 7 DVD's ISO image by running the following:

    ```
    ~]# umount /mnt
    ```

5. Next, remove the isolinux.cfg file using the following command:

    ```
    ~]# rm -f /root/iso/isolinux/isolinux.cfg
    ```

6. Create a new isolinux.cfg file, as follows:

    ```
    default vesamenu.c32
    timeout 600
    display boot.msg
    menu clear
    menu background splash.png
    menu title Red Hat Enterprise Linux 7.0
    menu vshift 8
    menu rows 18
    menu margin 8
    menu helpmsgrow 15
    menu tabmsgrow 13
    menu color sel 0 #ffffffff #00000000 none
    menu color title 0 #ffcc000000 #00000000 none
    menu color tabmsg 0 #84cc0000 #00000000 none
    menu color hotsel 0 #84cc0000 #00000000 none
    menu color hotkey 0 #ffffffff #00000000 none
    menu color cmdmark 0 #84b8ffff #00000000 none
    menu color cmdline 0 #ffffffff #00000000 none
    label linux
      menu label ^Install Red Hat Enterprise Linux 7.0
      kernel vmlinuz
      append initrd=initrd.img ks=http://kickstart.critter.be/
    kickstart.ks text

    label local
      menu label Boot from ^local drive
      localboot 0xffff

    menu end
    ```

7. Now, create the ISO by executing the following command:

```
~]# cd /root/iso

~/iso]# mkisofs -o ../boot.iso -b isolinux/isolinux.bin -c
isolinux/boot.cat -no-emul-boot -boot-load-size 4 -boot-info-table
-J -r .
```

More information on the options used with the `mkisofs` command can be found in the man pages for *mkisofs(1)*.

The following image shows the progress on creating a custom ISO:

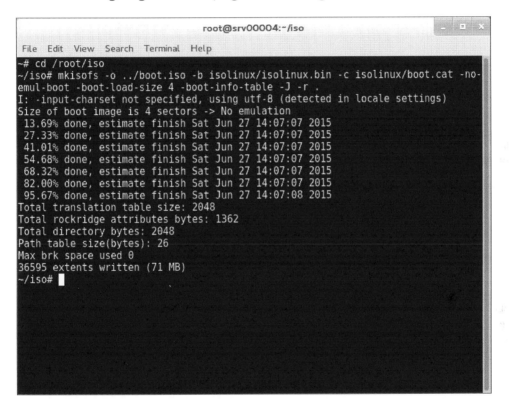

8. Then, use the ISO to install a guest on a KVM server, as shown in the following commands:

```
~]# virsh vol-create-as --pool localfs-vm --name rhel7_guest-da.
qcows2 --format qcows2 -capacity 10G

~]# virt-install \

--hvm \

--name rhel7_guest \
```

```
--memory 2G,maxmemory=4G \

--vcpus 2,max=4 \

--os-type linux \

--os-variant rhel7 \

--boot hd,cdrom,network,menu=on \

--controller type=scsi,model=virtio-scsi \

--disk device=cdrom,vol=iso/boot.iso,readonly=on,bus=scsi \

--disk device=disk,vol=localfs-vm/rhel7_guest-vda.
qcow2,cache=none,bus=scsi \

--network network=bridge-eth0,model=virtio \

--graphics vnc \

--graphics spice \

--noautoconsole \

--memballoon virtio
```

The following screenshot shows the console when booted with the custom ISO image:

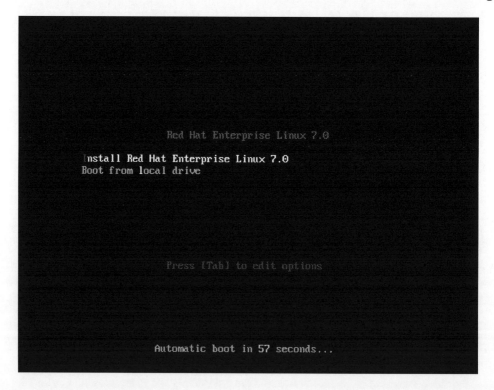

How it works...

Using the RHEL 7 installation media, we created a new boot ISO that allows us to install a new system. The ISO can be used to either burn a CD, with the dd tool to be copied on a USB stick, or to mount as virtual media. The way to mount this ISO as virtual media is different on each hardware platform, so this recipe shows you how to install it using KVM.

3
Configuring Your Network

The recipes we'll be covering in this chapter are as follows:

- ► Creating a VLAN interface
- ► Creating a teamed interface
- ► Creating a bridge
- ► Configuring IPv4 settings
- ► Configuring your DNS resolvers
- ► Configuring static network routes

Introduction

This chapter will attempt to explain how to use `NetworkManager`, which is the default network configuration tool and daemon in RHEL 7. It is a set of tools that makes networking simple and straightforward.

Configuring your network can be hard at times, especially when using the more exotic configuration options in combination with well-known configuration scripts. The `NetworkManager` allows you to easily configure your network without needing to edit the configuration files manually.

You can still edit the network configuration files located in `/etc/sysconfig/network-scripts` using your preferred editor; however, by default, `NetworkManager` does not notice any changes you make. You'll need to execute the following after editing the files located in the preceding location:

`~]# nmcli connection reload`

This is not enough to apply the changes immediately. You'll need to bring down and up the connection or reboot the system.

Alternatively, you can edit `/etc/NetworkManager/NetworkManager.conf` and add `monitor-connection-files=yes` to the `[main]` section. This will cause `NetworkManager` to pick up the changes and apply them immediately.

Within these recipes, you will get an overview on how to configure your network using the `NetworkManager` tools (`nmcli` and `nmtui`) and kickstart files.

Creating a VLAN interface

VLANs are isolated broadcast domains that run over a single physical network. They allow you to segment a local network and also to "stretch" a LAN over multiple physical locations. Most enterprises implement this on their network switching environment, but in some cases, the tagged VLANs reach your server.

Getting ready

In order to configure a VLAN, we need an established network connection on the local network interface.

How to do it...

For the sake of ease, our physical network interface is called `eth0`. The VLAN's ID is 1, and the IPv4 address is `10.0.0.2`, with a subnet mask of `255.0.0.0` and a default gateway of `10.0.0.1`.

Creating the VLAN connection with nmcli

With `nmcli`, we need to first create the connection and then activate it. Perform the following steps:

1. Create a VLAN interface using the following command:

   ~]# nmcli connection add type vlan dev eth0 id 1 ip4 10.0.0.2/8 gw4 10.0.0.1

   Connection 'vlan' (4473572d-26c0-49b8-a1a4-c20b485dad0d) successfully added.

   ~]#

2. Now, via this command, activate the connection:

   ~]# nmcli connection up vlan

   Connection successfully activated (D-Bus active path: /org/freedesktop/NetworkManager/ActiveConnection/7)

   ~]#

3. Check your network connection, as follows:

   ~]# nmcli connection show

   ~]# nmcli device status

   ~]# nmcli device show eth0.1

   Here is an example output of the preceding commands:

```
~]# nmcli connection show
NAME          UUID                                    TYPE            DEVICE
vlan          778fe568-2d9c-469b-99a1-6bba733baa2c    vlan            eth0.1
System eth0   05b32d2d-5298-406a-bc05-86316ed99583    802-3-ethernet  eth0
~]#
~]# nmcli device status
DEVICE    TYPE      STATE       CONNECTION
eth0      ethernet  connected   System eth0
eth0.1    vlan      connected   vlan
lo        loopback  unmanaged   --
~]#
~]# nmcli d show eth0.1
GENERAL.DEVICE:                    eth0.1
GENERAL.TYPE:                      vlan
GENERAL.HWADDR:                    52:54:00:F6:42:F3
GENERAL.MTU:                       1500
GENERAL.STATE:                     100 (connected)
GENERAL.CONNECTION:                vlan
GENERAL.CON-PATH:                  /org/freedesktop/NetworkManager/ActiveConnection/1
IP4.ADDRESS[1]:                    10.0.0.2/8
IP4.GATEWAY:                       10.0.0.1
IP6.ADDRESS[1]:                    fe80::5054:ff:fef6:42f3/64
IP6.GATEWAY:
~]#
```

Creating the VLAN connection with nmtui

The `nmtui` tool is a text user interface to `NetworkManager` and is launched by executing the following in a terminal:

```
~]# nmtui
```

This will bring up the following text-based interface:

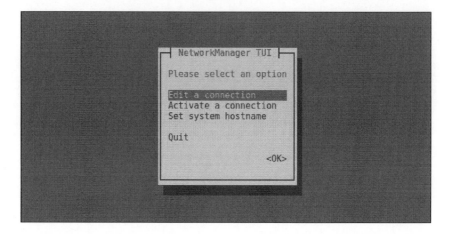

Navigation is done using the *Tab* and arrow keys, and the selection is done by pressing the *Enter* key. Now, you need to do the following:

1. Go to **Edit a connection** and select **<OK>**. The following screen will appear:

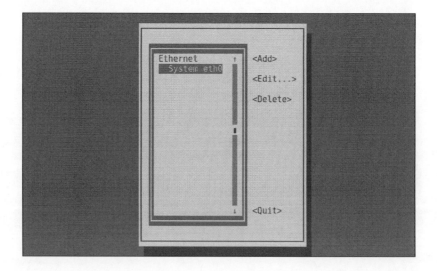

2. Next, select **<Add>** and the **VLAN** option. Confirm by Selecting **<Create>**:

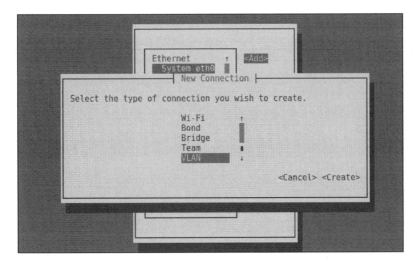

3. Enter the requested information in the following form and commit by selecting **<OK>**:

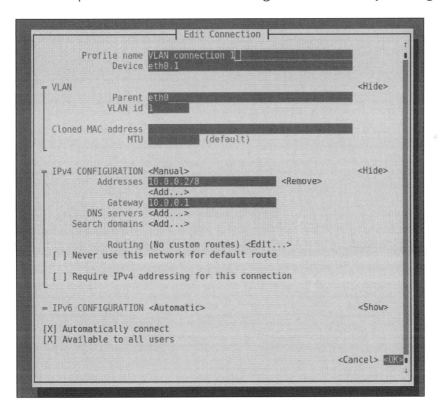

Your new **VLAN** interface will now be listed in the connections list:

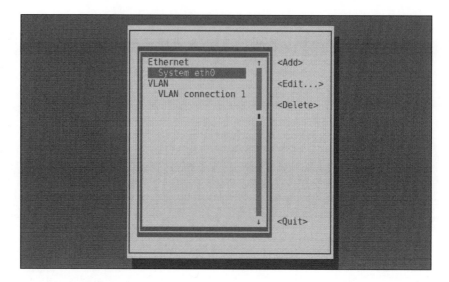

Creating the VLAN connection with kickstart

Let's explore what you need to add to your `kickstart` script in order to achieve the same result as in the preceding section:

1. Look for the configuration parameters within your `kickstart` file with the following command:

   ```
   . . .
   network --device=eth0
   . . .
   ```

2. Replace it with the following configuration parameters:

   ```
   network --device=eth0 --vlanid=1 --bootproto=static --
   ip=10.0.0.2 --netmask=255.0.0.0 --gateway=10.0.0.1
   ```

There's more...

The command line to create a VLAN with `nmcli` is pretty basic as it uses default values for every piece of information that is missing. To make sure that everything is created to your wishes, it is wise to also use `con-name` and `ifname`. These will respectively name your connection and the device you're creating. Take a look at the following command:

```
~]# nmcli connection add type vlan con-name vlan1 ifname eth0.1 dev eth0
id 1 ip4 10.0.0.2/8 gw4 10.0.0.1
```

This will create the `vlan.1` connection with `eth0` as the parent and `eth0.1` as the target device.

As with `nmcli` and `nmtui`, you can name your VLAN connection in `kickstart`; you only need to specify the `--interfacename` option. If you cannot find any previous network configuration in your `kickstart` file, just add the code to your `kickstart` file.

See also

The `nmcli` tool lacks a man page, but execute the following command for for more options to create VLAN connections:

```
~]# nmcli con add help
```

For more `kickstart` information on networks, check the following URL: `https://access.redhat.com/documentation/en-US/Red_Hat_Enterprise_Linux/7/html/Installation_Guide/sect-kickstart-syntax.html`.

Creating a teamed interface

Interface teaming, interface bonding, and link aggregation are all the same. It was already implemented in the kernel by way of the `bonding` driver. The team driver provides a different mechanism (from bonding) to team multiple network interfaces into a single logical one.

Getting ready

To set up a teamed interface, we'll need more than one network interface.

How to do it...

For the sake of ease, our physical network interfaces are called `eth1` and `eth2`. The IPv4 address for the team interface is `10.0.0.2`, with a subnet mask of `255.0.0.0` and a default gateway of `10.0.0.1`.

Creating the teamed interface using nmcli

Using this approach, we'll need to create the team connection and two team slaves and activate the connection, as follows:

1. Use the following command line to create the team connection:

   ```
   ~]# nmcli connection add type team ip4 10.0.0.2/8 gw4 10.0.0.1
   Connection 'team' (cfa46865-deb0-49f2-9156-4ca5461971b4)
   successfully added.
   ~]#
   ```

2. Add `eth1` to the team by executing the following:

    ```
    ~]# nmcli connection add type team-slave ifname eth1 master team
    ```

    ```
    Connection 'team-slave-eth1' (01880e55-f9a5-477b-b194-
    73278ef3dce5) successfully added.
    ```

    ```
    ~]#
    ```

3. Now, add `eth2` to the team by running the following command:

    ```
    ~]# nmcli connection add type team-slave ifname eth2 master team
    ```

    ```
    Connection 'team-slave-eth2' (f9efd19a-905f-4538-939c-
    3ea7516c3567) successfully added.
    ```

    ```
    ~]#
    ```

4. Bring the team up, as follows:

    ```
    ~]# nmcli connection up team
    ```

    ```
    Connection successfully activated (master waiting for
    slaves) (D-Bus active path: /org/freedesktop/NetworkManager/
    ActiveConnection/12)
    ```

    ```
    ~]#
    ```

5. Finally, check your network connections through the following commands:

    ```
    ~]# nmcli connection show
    ```

    ```
    ~]# nmcli device status
    ```

    ```
    ~]# nmcli device show nm-team
    ```

    Here's an example output of the preceding commands:

```
~]# nmcli c s
NAME              UUID                                    TYPE           DEVICE
team              fecca686-3d5f-4a61-8fe0-adce4b9a4368    team           nm-team
System eth0       05b32d2d-5298-406a-bc05-86316ed99583    802-3-ethernet eth0
team-slave-eth2   23ce3bc3-ab50-4962-9739-f7d2657afd91    802-3-ethernet eth2
team-slave-eth1   1ef26a49-60c2-4c8c-8772-550c4c3c690b    802-3-ethernet eth1
~]#
~]# nmcli d s
DEVICE     TYPE      STATE        CONNECTION
eth0       ethernet  connected    System eth0
eth1       ethernet  connected    team-slave-eth1
eth2       ethernet  connected    team-slave-eth2
nm-team    team      connected    team
lo         loopback  unmanaged    --
~]#
~]# nmcli d show nm-team
GENERAL.DEVICE:                    nm-team
GENERAL.TYPE:                      team
GENERAL.HWADDR:                    52:54:00:F6:42:F4
GENERAL.MTU:                       1500
GENERAL.STATE:                     100 (connected)
GENERAL.CONNECTION:                team
GENERAL.CON-PATH:                  /org/freedesktop/NetworkManager/ActiveConnection/6
IP4.ADDRESS[1]:                    10.0.0.2/8
IP4.GATEWAY:                       10.0.0.1
IP6.ADDRESS[1]:                    fe80::5054:ff:fef6:42f4/64
IP6.GATEWAY:
~]#
```

Creating the teamed interface using nmtui

Let's fire up `nmtui` and add a connection through the following steps:

1. First, create a team connection by selecting **<Add>**:

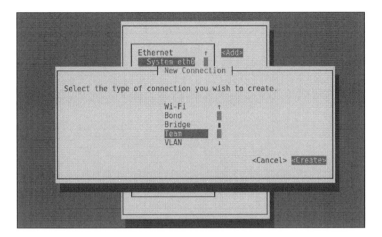

2. Enter the requested information in the following form and click on **<Add>** for every interface to add:

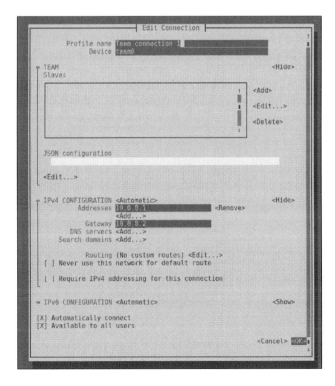

3. Next, select **<Add>** within team slaves to add an interface by filling out the form and selecting **<OK>**. Repeat this for every physical interface:

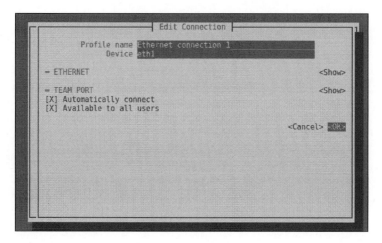

4. Now, select **<OK>** to create the team interface:

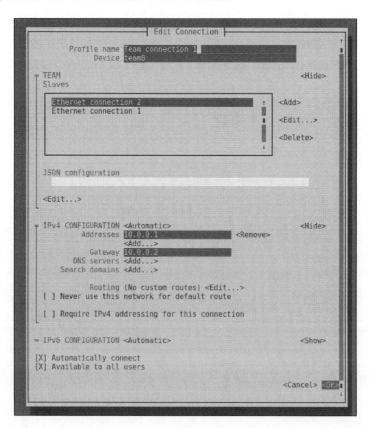

Your new team interface will now be listed in the connections list, as shown in the following screenshot:

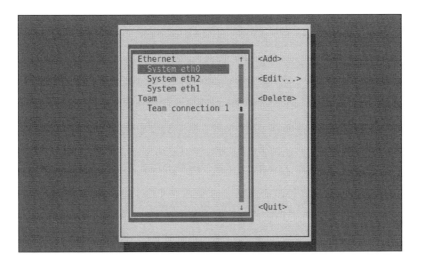

Creating the teamed interface with kickstart

Open your `kickstart` file with your favorite editor and perform the following steps:

1. Look for the network configuration parameters within your `kickstart` file by running the following command:

    ```
    ...
    network --device=eth0
    ...
    ```

2. Next, add the following configuration parameters:

    ```
    network --device=team0 --teamslaves="eth1,eth2" --
    bootproto=static --ip=10.0.0.2 --netmask=255.0.0.0 --
    gateway=10.0.0.1
    ```

There's more...

Teaming comes with runners—a way of load-sharing backup methods that you can assign to your team:

- ▶ **active-backup**: In this, one physical interface is used, while the others are kept as backup
- ▶ **broadcast**: In this, data is transmitted over all physical interfaces' selectors

- ▶ **LACP**: This implements `802.3ad` Link Aggregation Control Protocol
- ▶ **loadbalance**: This performs active Tx load balancing and uses a BPF-based Tx port
- ▶ **round-robin**: The data is transmitted over all physical interfaces in turn

These can also be defined upon creation using either of the presented options here:

nmcli

Add `team.config "{\"runner\":{\"name\": \"activebackup\"}}"` to your command to create your team interface, and substitute `activebackup` with the runner that you wish to use.

nmtui

Fill out the JSON configuration field for the team interface with `{"runner": {"name": "activebackup"}}`, and substitute `activebackup` with the runner that you wish to use.

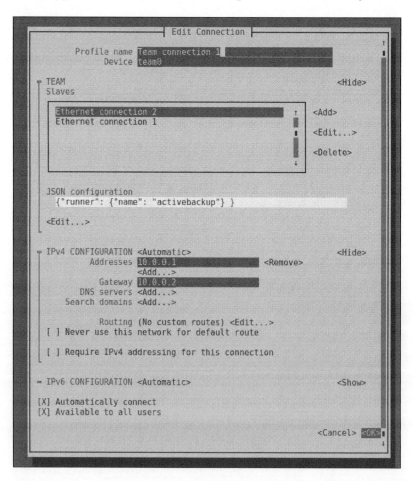

kickstart

Add `--teamconfig="{\"runner\":{\"name\": \"activebackup\"}}"` to your team device line, and substitute `activebackup` with the runner that you wish to use.

The options provided to create the team interface are bare bones using `nmcli`. If you wish to add a connection and interface name, use `con-name` and `ifname`, respectively, in this way:

```
~]# nmcli connection add type team con-name team0 ifname team0 ip4
10.0.0.2/8 gw4 10.0.0.1
Connection 'team0' (e1856313-ecd4-420e-96d5-c76bc00794aa) successfully
added.
~]#
```

The same is true for adding the team slaves, except for `ifname`, which is required to specify the correct interface:

```
~# nmcli connection add type team-slave con-name team0-slave0 ifname eth1
master team0
Connection 'team0-slave0' (3cb2f603-1f73-41a0-b476-7a356d4b6274)
successfully added.
~# nmcli connection add type team-slave con-name team0-slave1 ifname eth2
master team0
Connection 'team0-slave1' (074e4dd3-8a3a-4997-b444-a781114c58c9)
successfully added.
~#
```

See also

For more information on the networking team daemon and "runners", refer to the following URL:

```
https://access.redhat.com/documentation/en-US/Red_Hat_Enterprise_
Linux/7/html/Networking_Guide/sec-Understanding_the_Network_Teaming_
Daemon_and_the_Runners.html
```

For more information on using `nmcli` to create team interfaces, take a look at the following link:

```
https://access.redhat.com/documentation/en-US/Red_Hat_Enterprise_
Linux/7/html/Networking_Guide/sec-Configure_a_Network_Team_Using-the_
Command_Line.html
```

For more information on using `nmtui` to create team interfaces, follow this link:

```
https://access.redhat.com/documentation/en-US/Red_Hat_Enterprise_
Linux/7/html/Networking_Guide/sec-Configure_a_Network_Team_Using_the_
Text_User_Interface_nmtui.html
```

For more information on creating team interfaces in kickstart scripts, the following link will be useful:

```
https://access.redhat.com/documentation/en-US/Red_Hat_Enterprise_
Linux/7/html/Installation_Guide/sect-kickstart-syntax.html
```

Creating a bridge

A network bridge is a logical device that forwards traffic between connected physical interfaces based on MAC addresses. This kind of bridge can be used to emulate a hardware bridge in virtualization applications, such as KVM, to share the NIC with multiple virtual NICs.

Getting ready

To bridge two physical networks, we need two network interfaces. Your physical interfaces should never be configured with any address as the bridge will be configured with the IP address(es).

How to do it...

For the sake of ease, the physical network interfaces we will bridge are `eth1` and `eth2`. The IPv4 address will be `10.0.0.2` with a subnet mask of `255.0.0.0` and a default gateway of `10.0.0.1`.

Creating a bridge using nmcli

Make sure that you activate the bridge after configuring the bridge and interfaces! Here are the steps that you need to perform for this:

1. First, create the bridge connection via the following command:

   ```
   ~]# nmcli connection add type bridge ip4 10.0.0.2/8 gw4 10.0.0.1
   Connection 'bridge' (36e40910-cf6a-4a6c-ae28-c0d6fb90954d)
   successfully added.
   ~]#
   ```

2. Add `eth1` to the bridge, as follows:

   ```
   ~]# nmcli connection add type bridge-slave ifname eth1 master
   bridge
   Connection 'bridge-slave-eth1' (6821a067-f25c-46f6-89d4-
   a318fc4db683) successfully added.
   ~]#
   ```

3. Next, add `eth2` to the bridge using the following command:

   ```
   ~]# nmcli connection add type bridge-slave ifname eth2 master
   bridge
   Connection 'bridge-slave-eth2' (f20d0a7b-da03-4338-8060-
   07a3775772f4) successfully added.
   ~]#
   ```

4. Activate the bridge by executing the following:

   ```
   ~# nmcli connection up bridge
   Connection successfully activated (master waiting for
   slaves) (D-Bus active path: /org/freedesktop/NetworkManager/
   ActiveConnection/30)
   ~]#
   ```

5. Now, check your network connection by running the following commands:

   ```
   ~]# nmcli connection show
   ~]# nmcli device status
   ~]# nmcli device show bridge
   ```

   Here is an example output of the preceding commands:

```
~]# nmcli connection show
NAME               UUID                                   TYPE            DEVICE
System eth0        05b32d2d-5298-406a-bc05-86316ed99583   802-3-ethernet  eth0
bridge-slave-eth2  96203d35-1d55-4366-8110-b7b4c0becc2b   802-3-ethernet  eth2
bridge-slave-eth1  e49b4127-cc2a-4710-86bc-a12220fa85ca   802-3-ethernet  eth1
bridge             4cef8132-1f93-4936-af45-ea2f01c95246   bridge          nm-bridge
~]#
~]# nmcli device status
DEVICE     TYPE      STATE       CONNECTION
nm-bridge  bridge    connected   bridge
eth0       ethernet  connected   System eth0
eth1       ethernet  connected   bridge-slave-eth1
eth2       ethernet  connected   bridge-slave-eth2
lo         loopback  unmanaged   --
~]#
~]# nmcli device show nm-bridge
GENERAL.DEVICE:          nm-bridge
GENERAL.TYPE:            bridge
GENERAL.HWADDR:          52:54:00:F6:42:F4
GENERAL.MTU:             1500
GENERAL.STATE:           100 (connected)
GENERAL.CONNECTION:      bridge
GENERAL.CON-PATH:        /org/freedesktop/NetworkManager/ActiveConnection/12
IP4.ADDRESS[1]:          10.0.0.2/8
IP4.GATEWAY:             10.0.0.1
IP6.ADDRESS[1]:          fe80::5054:ff:fef6:42f4/64
IP6.GATEWAY:
~]#
```

Creating a bridge using nmtui

Launch `nmtui` and select **Edit a connection**. After this, follow these steps to create a bridge using `nmtui`:

1. Create a bridge connection by selecting **<Add>** and **Bridge** from the connection list and then click on **<Create>**:

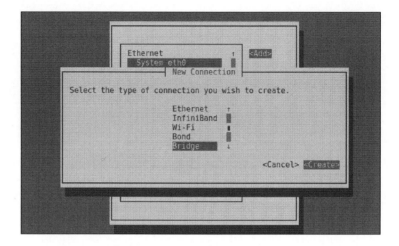

2. Fill out the presented form with the required information:

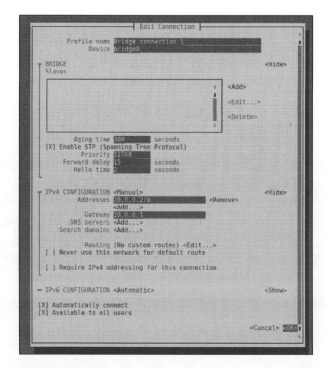

3. Next, add the two network interfaces by selecting **<Add>** and providing the requested information for each interface:

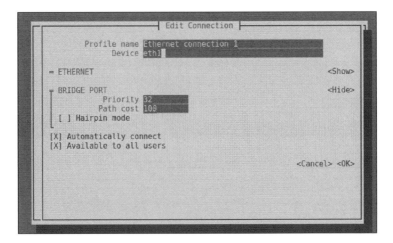

4. Finally, select **<OK>** to create the bridge:

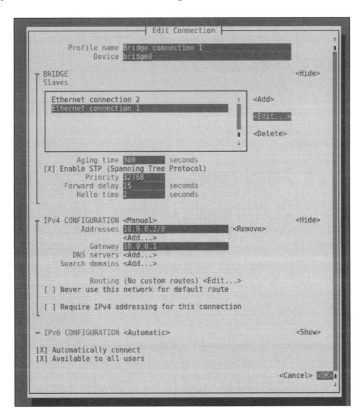

Your new bridge will now be listed in the connections list:

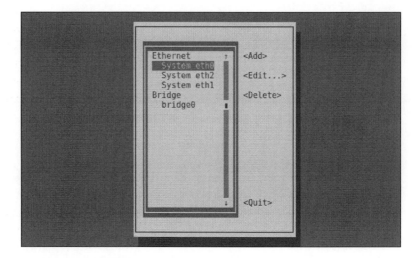

Creating a bridge with kickstart

Edit your `kickstart` file with your favorite editor through the following steps:

1. Look for the configuration parameters within your `kickstart` file using this command line:

    ```
    . . .
    network --device=eth0
    . . .
    ```

2. Now, add the following configuration parameters:

    ```
    network --device=bridge0 --bridgeslaves="eth1,eth2" --
    bootproto=static --ip=10.0.0.2 --netmask=255.0.0.0 --
    gateway=10.0.0.1
    ```

There's more...

The options provided to create the bridge are bare bones using `nmcli`. If you wish to add a connection and interface name, use `con-name` and `ifname`, respectively, in this way:

```
~# nmcli connection add type bridge con-name bridge0 ifname bridge0 ip4
10.0.0.2/8 gw4 10.0.0.1
```

```
Connection 'bridge0' (d04180be-3e80-4bd4-a0fe-b26d79d71c7d) successfully
added.
```

```
~#
```

The same is true for adding the bridge slaves, except for `ifname`, which is required to specify the correct interface:

```
~]# nmcli connection add type bridge-slave con-name bridge0-slave0 ifname
eth1 master bridge0
Connection 'bridge0-slave0' (3a885ca5-6ffb-42a3-9044-83c6142f1967)
successfully added.
~]# nmcli connection add type team-slave con-name team0-slave1 ifname
eth2 master team0
Connection 'bridge0-slave1' (f79716f1-7b7f-4462-87d9-6801eee1952f)
successfully added.
~]#
```

See also

For more information on creating network bridges using `nmcli`, go to the following URL:

```
https://access.redhat.com/documentation/en-US/Red_Hat_Enterprise_
Linux/7/html/Networking_Guide/sec-Network_Bridging_Using_the_
NetworkManager_Command_Line_Tool_nmcli.html
```

For more information on creating network bridges using `nmtui`, go to this website:

```
https://access.redhat.com/documentation/en-US/Red_Hat_Enterprise_
Linux/7/html/Networking_Guide/ch-Configure_Network_Bridging.html
```

For more information on kickstart and bridging, go to the following website:

```
https://access.redhat.com/documentation/en-US/Red_Hat_Enterprise_
Linux/7/html/Installation_Guide/sect-kickstart-syntax.html
```

Configuring IPv4 settings

Changing your IP addresses is pretty straightforward in the old `ifcfg`-style files, and it's actually pretty simple using `NetworkManager` tools as well.

As kickstart is only used to set up a system, it is not relevant to go in depth into this matter in this recipe.

How to do it...

Let's change our current IPv4 address and gateway for `eth1` to `10.0.0.3/8`, with `10.0.0.2` as the default gateway.

Setting your IPv4 configuration using nmcli

Perform the following steps:

1. Set the ipv4 information by executing the following command line:

   ```
   ~]# nmcli connection modify eth0 ipv4.addresses 10.0.0.3/8 ipv4.
   gateway 10.0.0.2
   ```

2. Now, run the following to verify the information:

   ```
   ~]# nmcli connection show eth0
   ```

   Here is an example output of the preceding commands:

```
~]# nmcli connection show eth0
connection.id:                          eth0
connection.uuid:                        05b32d2d-5298-406a-bc05-86316ed99583
connection.interface-name:              eth0
connection.type:                        802-3-ethernet
connection.autoconnect:                 yes
connection.autoconnect-priority:        0
connection.timestamp:                   1446020183
connection.read-only:                   no
connection.permissions:
connection.zone:                        --
connection.master:                      --
connection.slave-type:                  --
connection.secondaries:
connection.gateway-ping-timeout:        0
802-3-ethernet.port:                    --
802-3-ethernet.speed:                   0
802-3-ethernet.duplex:                  --
802-3-ethernet.auto-negotiate:          yes
802-3-ethernet.mac-address:             52:54:00:F6:42:F3
802-3-ethernet.cloned-mac-address:      --
802-3-ethernet.mac-address-blacklist:
802-3-ethernet.mtu:                     auto
802-3-ethernet.s390-subchannels:
802-3-ethernet.s390-nettype:            --
802-3-ethernet.s390-options:
ipv4.method:                            manual
ipv4.dns:
ipv4.dns-search:                        example.com
ipv4.addresses:                         10.0.0.3/8
ipv4.gateway:                           10.0.0.2
ipv4.routes:
ipv4.route-metric:                      -1
ipv4.ignore-auto-routes:                no
ipv4.ignore-auto-dns:                   no
ipv4.dhcp-client-id:                    --
ipv4.dhcp-send-hostname:                yes
ipv4.dhcp-hostname:                     --
ipv4.never-default:                     no
ipv4.may-fail:                          yes
ipv6.method:                            auto
ipv6.dns:
ipv6.dns-search:
ipv6.addresses:
ipv6.gateway:                           --
ipv6.routes:
ipv6.route-metric:                      -1
ipv6.ignore-auto-routes:                no
ipv6.ignore-auto-dns:                   no
ipv6.never-default:                     no
ipv6.may-fail:                          yes
ipv6.ip6-privacy:                       -1 (unknown)
ipv6.dhcp-send-hostname:                yes
ipv6.dhcp-hostname:                     --
GENERAL.NAME:                           eth0
GENERAL.UUID:                           05b32d2d-5298-406a-bc05-86316ed99583
GENERAL.DEVICES:                        eth0
GENERAL.STATE:                          activated
GENERAL.DEFAULT:                        yes
GENERAL.DEFAULT6:                       no
GENERAL.VPN:                            no
GENERAL.ZONE:                           --
GENERAL.DBUS-PATH:                      /org/freedesktop/NetworkManager/ActiveConnection/0
GENERAL.CON-PATH:                       /org/freedesktop/NetworkManager/Settings/1
GENERAL.SPEC-OBJECT:                    /
GENERAL.MASTER-PATH:                    --
IP4.ADDRESS[1]:                         10.0.0.3/8
IP4.GATEWAY:                            10.0.0.2
IP6.ADDRESS[1]:                         fe80::5054:ff:fef6:42f3/64
IP6.GATEWAY:
~]#
```

Setting your IPv4 configuration using nmtui

The `nmtui` tool takes a bit more work, but the end result remains the same. Perform the following steps:

1. Start `nmtui`, select the interface that you wish to modify, and click on **<Edit...>**:

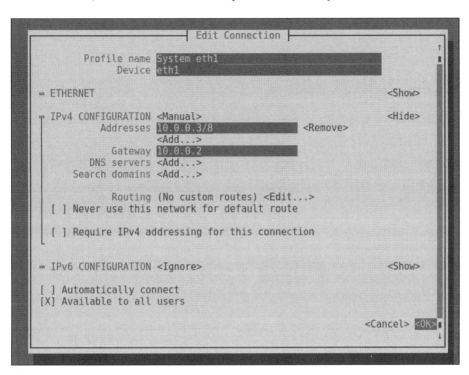

2. Now, modify the IPv4 configuration to your liking and click on **<OK>**.

There's more...

Managing IPv6 ip addresses is as straightforward as configuring your IPv4 counterparts.

The options you need to use in kickstart to set your ip address and gateway are:

- ▶ `--ip`: This is used to set the system's IPv4 address
- ▶ `--netmask`: This is used for the subnet mask
- ▶ `--gateway`: This is used to set the IPv4 gateway

Configuring your DNS resolvers

DNS servers are stored in `/etc/resolv.conf`. You can also manage this file using `NetworkManager`.

As with the previous recipe, and for the same reasons, this recipe won't go into the `kickstart` options.

How to do it...

Let's set the DNS resolvers for `eth1` to point to Google's public DNS servers: `8.8.8.8` and `8.8.4.4`.

Setting your DNS resolvers using nmcli

Perform the following steps:

1. Set the DNS servers via the following command:

   ```
   ~]# nmcli connection modify System\ eth1 ipv4.dns
   "8.8.8.8,8.8.4.4"
   ```

2. Now, use the following command to check your configuration:

   ```
   ~]# nmcli connection show System\ eth1
   ```

Here is an example output of the preceding commands:

```
~]# nmcli c s System\ eth0
connection.id:                              System eth0
connection.uuid:                            05b32d2d-5298-406a-bc05-86316ed99583
connection.interface-name:                  eth0
connection.type:                            802-3-ethernet
connection.autoconnect:                     yes
connection.autoconnect-priority:            0
connection.timestamp:                       1446820783
connection.read-only:                       no
connection.permissions:
connection.zone:                            --
connection.master:                          --
connection.slave-type:                      --
connection.secondaries:
connection.gateway-ping-timeout:            0
802-3-ethernet.port:                        --
802-3-ethernet.speed:                       0
802-3-ethernet.duplex:                      --
802-3-ethernet.auto-negotiate:              yes
802-3-ethernet.mac-address:                 52:54:00:F6:42:F3
802-3-ethernet.cloned-mac-address:          --
802-3-ethernet.mac-address-blacklist:
802-3-ethernet.mtu:                         auto
802-3-ethernet.s390-subchannels:
802-3-ethernet.s390-nettype:                --
802-3-ethernet.s390-options:
ipv4.method:                                manual
ipv4.dns:                                   8.8.8.8,8.8.4.4
ipv4.dns-search:                            example.com
ipv4.addresses:                             10.0.0.3/8
ipv4.gateway:                               10.0.0.2
ipv4.routes:
ipv4.route-metric:                          -1
ipv4.ignore-auto-routes:                    no
ipv4.ignore-auto-dns:                       no
ipv4.dhcp-client-id:                        --
ipv4.dhcp-send-hostname:                    yes
ipv4.dhcp-hostname:                         --
ipv4.never-default:                         no
ipv4.may-fail:                              yes
ipv6.method:                                auto
ipv6.dns:
ipv6.dns-search:
ipv6.addresses:
ipv6.gateway:                               --
ipv6.routes:
ipv6.route-metric:                          -1
ipv6.ignore-auto-routes:                    no
ipv6.ignore-auto-dns:                       no
ipv6.never-default:                         no
ipv6.may-fail:                              yes
ipv6.ip6-privacy:                           -1 (unknown)
ipv6.dhcp-send-hostname:                    yes
ipv6.dhcp-hostname:                         --
GENERAL.NAME:                               System eth0
GENERAL.UUID:                               05b32d2d-5298-406a-bc05-86316ed99583
GENERAL.DEVICES:                            eth0
GENERAL.STATE:                              activated
GENERAL.DEFAULT:                            yes
GENERAL.DEFAULT6:                           no
GENERAL.VPN:                                no
GENERAL.ZONE:                               --
GENERAL.DBUS-PATH:                          /org/freedesktop/NetworkManager/ActiveConnection/0
GENERAL.CON-PATH:                           /org/freedesktop/NetworkManager/Settings/1
GENERAL.SPEC-OBJECT:                        /
GENERAL.MASTER-PATH:                        --
IP4.ADDRESS[1]:                             10.0.0.3/8
IP4.GATEWAY:                                10.0.0.2
IP6.ADDRESS[1]:                             fe80::5054:ff:fef6:42f3/64
IP6.GATEWAY:
~]#
```

Setting your DNS resolvers using nmtui

The nmtui tool requires a bit more work to set the DNS resolvers, as follows:

1. Start nmtui, select the interface that you wish to modify, and click on **<Edit...>**:

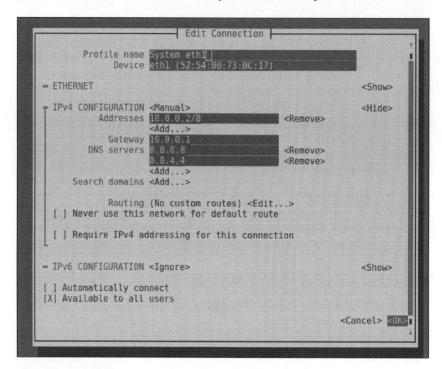

There's more...

The nmcli tool supports adding multiple DNS servers by separating them with a semicolon. Using a blank value (" ") will remove all the DNS servers for this connection.

Similarly, you can set the DNS search domains for your environment. When using nmcli, you'll need to specify the ipv4.dns-search property.

Kickstart will allow you to specify the DNS servers using the --nameserver option for each DNS server. If you do not wish to specify any DNS servers, use --nodns. Unfortunately, there is no native way to set the DNS domain search using kickstart. You will have to use nmcli, for example, in the %post section of your kickstart script.

 Be careful when setting DNS configurations for multiple network interfaces. NetworkManager adds all your nameservers to your resolv.conf file, but libc may not support more than six nameservers.

Configuring static network routes

In some cases, it is required to set static routes on your system. As static routes are not natively supported in kickstart, this is not covered in this recipe.

How to do it...

Add static routes to both the 192.168.0.0/24 and 192.168.1.0/24 networks via 10.0.0.1.

Configuring static network routes using nmcli

Here's what you need to do:

1. Set the route using the following command:

```
~]# nmcli connection modify eth0 ipv4.routes "192.168.0.0/24
10.0.0.1,192.168.1.0/24 10.0.0.1"
```

2. Now, execute the following command line to verify the configuration:

```
~]# nmcli connection show eth0
```

Here is an example output of the preceding commands:

```
~]# nmcli connection show eth0
connection.id:                          eth0
connection.uuid:                        05b32d2d-5298-406a-bc05-86316ed99583
connection.interface-name:              eth0
connection.type:                        802-3-ethernet
connection.autoconnect:                 yes
connection.autoconnect-priority:        0
connection.timestamp:                   1446821383
connection.read-only:                   no
connection.permissions:
connection.zone:                        --
connection.master:                      --
connection.slave-type:                  --
connection.secondaries:
connection.gateway-ping-timeout:        0
802-3-ethernet.port:                    --
802-3-ethernet.speed:                   0
802-3-ethernet.duplex:                  --
802-3-ethernet.auto-negotiate:          yes
802-3-ethernet.mac-address:             52:54:00:F6:42:F3
802-3-ethernet.cloned-mac-address:      --
802-3-ethernet.mac-address-blacklist:
802-3-ethernet.mtu:                     auto
802-3-ethernet.s390-subchannels:
802-3-ethernet.s390-nettype:            --
802-3-ethernet.s390-options:
ipv4.method:                            manual
ipv4.dns:                               8.8.8.8,8.8.4.4
ipv4.dns-search:                        example.com
ipv4.addresses:                         10.0.0.3/8
ipv4.gateway:                           10.0.0.2
ipv4.routes:                            { ip = 192.168.0.0/24, nh = 10.0.0.1 }; { ip = 192.168.1.0/24, nh = 10.0
.0.1 }
ipv4.route-metric:                      -1
ipv4.ignore-auto-routes:                no
ipv4.ignore-auto-dns:                   no
ipv4.dhcp-client-id:                    --
ipv4.dhcp-send-hostname:                yes
ipv4.dhcp-hostname:                     --
ipv4.never-default:                     no
ipv4.may-fail:                          yes
ipv6.method:                            auto
ipv6.dns:
ipv6.dns-search:
ipv6.addresses:
ipv6.gateway:                           --
ipv6.routes:
ipv6.route-metric:                      -1
ipv6.ignore-auto-routes:                no
ipv6.ignore-auto-dns:                   no
ipv6.never-default:                     no
ipv6.may-fail:                          yes
ipv6.ip6-privacy:                       -1 (unknown)
ipv6.dhcp-send-hostname:                yes
ipv6.dhcp-hostname:                     --
GENERAL.NAME:                           eth0
GENERAL.UUID:                           05b32d2d-5298-406a-bc05-86316ed99583
GENERAL.DEVICES:                        eth0
GENERAL.STATE:                          activated
GENERAL.DEFAULT:                        yes
GENERAL.DEFAULT6:                       no
GENERAL.VPN:                            no
GENERAL.ZONE:                           --
GENERAL.DBUS-PATH:                      /org/freedesktop/NetworkManager/ActiveConnection/0
GENERAL.CON-PATH:                       /org/freedesktop/NetworkManager/Settings/1
GENERAL.SPEC-OBJECT:                    /
GENERAL.MASTER-PATH:                    --
IP4.ADDRESS[1]:                         10.0.0.3/8
IP4.GATEWAY:                            10.0.0.2
IP6.ADDRESS[1]:                         fe80::5054:ff:fef6:42f3/64
IP6.GATEWAY:
~]#
```

Configuring network routes using nmtui

Here are the steps for this recipe:

1. Launch `nmtui`, select the interface that you wish to modify the static routes for, and click on **<Edit...>**:

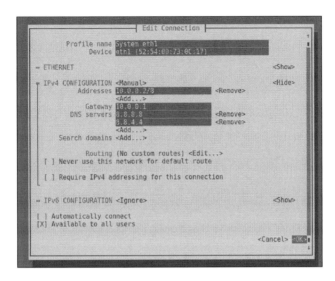

2. Now, select **<Edit...>** next to the **IPv4 Configuration – Routing** entry and enter your routes. Select **<OK>** to confirm:

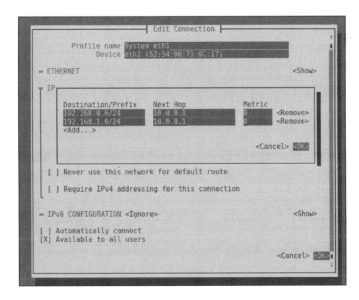

3. Finally, click on **<OK>** to confirm the changes and save them.

4

Configuring Your New System

Here's an overview of the recipes that we'll be covering in this chapter:

- ▶ The `systemd` service and setting runlevels
- ▶ Starting and stopping `systemd` services
- ▶ Configuring the `systemd` journal for persistence
- ▶ Monitoring services using `journalctl`
- ▶ Configuring `logrotate`
- ▶ Managing time
- ▶ Configuring your boot environment
- ▶ Configuring `smtp`

Introduction

Once your system is installed and the network is configured, it's time to start configuring everything else.

RHEL 7 comes with the `systemd init` daemon, which takes care of your daemon or service housekeeping and more, replacing the old SysV (UNIX System V) init system.

Its main advantages are automatic dependency handling, parallel startup of services, and the monitoring of started services with the ability to restart crashed services.

For a good read on `systemd` and its inner workings, head over to `https://n0where.net/understanding-systemd`.

The systemd service and setting runlevels

The `systemd` service doesn't use runlevels as SysV or Upstart do. The alternatives for `systemd` are called targets. Their purpose is to group a set of `systemd` units (not only services, but also sockets, devices, and so on) through a chain of dependencies.

How to do it...

Managing targets with `systemd` is pretty simple, as shown through the following steps:

1. List all target units, as follows:

```
~]# systemctl list-unit-files --type target
UNIT FILE               STATE
anaconda.target         static
basic.target            static
bluetooth.target        static
cryptsetup.target       static
ctrl-alt-del.target     disabled
default.target          enabled

...

sysinit.target          static
system-update.target    static
time-sync.target        static
timers.target           static
umount.target           static

58 unit files listed.
~]#
```

This list shows all target units available followed by information regarding whether the target is enabled or not.

2. Now, show the currently loaded target units.

The `systemd` targets can be chained unlike SysV runlevels, so you'll not only see one target but a whole bunch of them, as follows:

```
~]# systemctl list-units --type target
UNIT                    LOAD    ACTIVE SUB    DESCRIPTION
basic.target            loaded active active Basic System
```

```
cryptsetup.target        loaded active active Encrypted Volumes
getty.target             loaded active active Login Prompts
local-fs-pre.target      loaded active active Local File Systems
(Pre)
local-fs.target          loaded active active Local File Systems
multi-user.target        loaded active active Multi-User System
network-online.target loaded active active Network is Online
network.target           loaded active active Network
nfs-client.target        loaded active active NFS client services
paths.target             loaded active active Paths
remote-fs-pre.target     loaded active active Remote File Systems
(Pre)
remote-fs.target         loaded active active Remote File Systems
slices.target            loaded active active Slices
sockets.target           loaded active active Sockets
swap.target              loaded active active Swap
sysinit.target           loaded active active System Initialization
time-sync.target         loaded active active System Time
Synchronized
timers.target            loaded active active Timers


LOAD   = Reflects whether the unit definition was properly loaded.
ACTIVE = The high-level unit activation state, i.e. generalization
of SUB.
SUB    = The low-level unit activation state, values depend on
unit type.


18 loaded units listed. Pass --all to see loaded but inactive
units, too.
To show all installed unit files use 'systemctl list-unit-files'.
~]#
```

3. Next, change the default `systemd` target by running the following commands:

```
~]# systemctl set-default graphical.target
rm '/etc/systemd/system/default.target'
ln -s '/usr/lib/systemd/system/graphical.target' '/etc/systemd/
system/default.target'
~]#
```

There's more...

Sometimes, you want to change targets on the fly as you would in the past with runlevel or telinit. With `systemd`, this is accomplished in the following way:

```
~]# systemctl isolate <target name>
```

Here's an example:

```
~]# systemctl isolate graphical.target
```

Let's take an overview of the former runlevels versus the `systemd` targets in the following table:

Runlevel	Target units	Description
0	`runlevel0.target` or `poweroff.target`	This is used to shut down and power off the system
1	`runlevel1.target` or `rescue.target`	This is used to enter a rescue shell
2	`runlevel2.target` or `multi-user.target`	This is used to set up a command-line multiuser system
3	`runlevel3.target` or `multi-user.target`	This is used to set up a command-line multiuser system
4	`runlevel4.target` or `multi-user.target`	This is used to set up a command-line multiuser system
5	`runlevel5.target` or `graphical.target`	This is used to set up a graphical multiuser system
6	`runlevel6.target` or `reboot.target`	This is used to reboot the system

See also

For more in-depth information about RHEL 7 and `systemd` targets, refer to the following link: `https://access.redhat.com/documentation/en-US/Red_Hat_Enterprise_Linux/7/html/System_Administrators_Guide/sect-Managing_Services_with_systemd-Targets.html`

Starting and stopping systemd services

Although this recipe uses services by their base name, they can also be addressed by their full filename. For example, `sshd` can be substituted by `sshd.service`.

How to do it...

The following steps need to be performed to successfully start or stop `systemd` services:

1. List all available `systemd` services, as follows:

    ```
    ~]# systemctl list-unit-files --type service
    UNIT FILE                               STATE
    atd.service                             enabled
    auditd.service                          enabled
    auth-rpcgss-module.service              static
    autovt@.service                         disabled
    avahi-daemon.service                    disabled
    blk-availability.service                disabled
    brandbot.service                        static

    ...

    systemd-udev-trigger.service            static
    systemd-udevd.service                   static
    systemd-update-utmp-runlevel.service    static
    systemd-update-utmp.service             static
    systemd-user-sessions.service           static
    systemd-vconsole-setup.service          static
    tcsd.service                            disabled
    teamd@.service                          static
    tuned.service                           enabled
    wpa_supplicant.service                  disabled
    xinetd.service                          enabled

    161 unit files listed.
    ```

    This shows all service units available followed by information regarding whether the service is enabled or not.

2. Now, list all the loaded `systemd` services and their status, as follows:

    ```
    ~]# systemctl list-units --type service --all
    UNIT                    LOAD    ACTIVE   SUB      DESCRIPTION
    ```

```
atd.service                loaded active    running Job spooling
tools
auditd.service             loaded active    running Security
Auditing Service
auth-rpcgss-module.service loaded inactive dead    Kernel Module
supporting RPC
brandbot.service           loaded inactive dead    Flexible
Branding Service
cpupower.service           loaded inactive dead    Configure CPU
power related
crond.service              loaded active    running Command
Scheduler
cups.service               loaded inactive dead    CUPS Printing
Service
dbus.service               loaded active    running D-Bus System
Message Bus
...


systemd-...es-setup.service loaded active   exited  Create
Volatile Files and Di
systemd-...-trigger.service loaded active   exited  udev Coldplug
all Devices
systemd-udevd.service       loaded active   running udev Kernel
Device Manager
systemd-update-utmp.service loaded active   exited  Update UTMP
about System Reb
systemd-...sessions.service loaded active   exited  Permit User
Sessions
systemd-...le-setup.service loaded active   exited  Setup Virtual
Console
tuned.service              loaded active    running Dynamic System
Tuning Daemon
xinetd.service             loaded active    running Xinetd A
Powerful Replacemen
LOAD   = Reflects whether the unit definition was properly loaded.
ACTIVE = The high-level unit activation state, i.e. generalization
of SUB.
SUB    = The low-level unit activation state, values depend on
unit type.


103 loaded units listed.
```

```
To show all installed unit files use 'systemctl list-unit-files'.
~]#
```

3. Next, get the status of a service.

   To get the status of a particular service, execute the following, substituting `<service>` with the name of the service:

   ```
   ~]# systemctl status <service>
   ```

   Here's an example:

   ```
   ~]# systemctl status sshd
   sshd.service - OpenSSH server daemon
      Loaded: loaded (/usr/lib/systemd/system/sshd.service; enabled)
      Active: active (running) since Fri 2015-07-17 09:13:55 CEST; 1
   weeks 0 days ago
    Main PID: 11880 (sshd)
      CGroup: /system.slice/sshd.service
              └─11880 /usr/sbin/sshd -D


   Jul 22 12:07:31 rhel7.mydomain.lan sshd[10340]: Accepted publickey
   for root...
   Jul 22 12:12:29 rhel7.mydomain.lan sshd[10459]: Accepted publickey
   for root...
   Jul 22 12:13:33 rhel7.mydomain.lan sshd[10473]: Accepted publickey
   for root...
   Jul 24 21:27:24 rhel7.mydomain.lan sshd[28089]: Accepted publickey
   for root...
   Hint: Some lines were ellipsized, use -l to show in full.
   ~]#
   ```

4. Now, start and stop the systemd services.

   To stop a systemd service, execute the following, substituting `<service>` with the name of the service:

   ```
   ~]# systemctl stop <service>
   ```

   Here's an example:

   ```
   ~]# systemctl stop sshd
   ```

   To start a systemd service, execute the following, substituting `<service>` with the name of the service:

   ```
   ~]# systemctl start <service>
   ```

Here's an example:

```
~]# systemctl start sshd
```

5. Next, enable and disable the `systemd` services.

    To enable a `systemd` service, execute the following, substituting `<service>` with the name of the service:

    ```
    ~]# systemctl enable <service>
    ```

    Here's an example:

    ```
    ~]# systemctl enable sshd
    ln -s '/usr/lib/systemd/system/sshd.service' '/etc/systemd/system/
    multi-user.target.wants/sshd.service'
    ~]#
    ```

    To disable a `systemd` service, execute the following, substituting `<service>` with the name of the service:

    ```
    ~]# systemctl disable <service>
    ```

    Here's an example:

    ```
    ~]# systemctl disable sshd
    rm '/etc/systemd/system/multi-user.target.wants/sshd.service'
    ~]#
    ```

6. Now, configure a service to restart when crashed.

    Let's make the `ntpd` service restart if it crashes after 1 minute.

    1. First, create the directory, as follows: `/etc/systemd/system/ntpd.service.d`.

        ```
        ~]# mkdir -p /etc/systemd/system/ntpd.service.d
        ```

    2. Create a new file in that directory named `restart.conf` and add the following to it:

        ```
        [Service]
        Restart=on-failure
        RestartSec=60s
        ```

    3. Next, reload the unit files and recreate the dependency tree using the following command:

        ```
        ~]# systemctl daemon-reload
        ```

    4. Finally, restart the `ntpd` service by executing the following command:

        ```
        ~]# systemctl restart ntpd
        ```

There's more...

When requesting the status of a service, the most recent log entries are also shown when executed as `root`.

The service status information can be seen in the following table:

Field	Description
Loaded	This provides information on whether the service is loaded and enabled. It also includes the absolute path to the service file.
Active	This provides information on whether the service is running, followed by the time it started.
Main PID	This provides PID of the corresponding service, followed by its name.
Status	This provides information about the corresponding service.
Process	This provides information about the related process.
Cgroup	This provides information about related control groups.

In some (rare) cases, you want to prevent a service from being started, either manually or by another service; there is an option to mask the service, which is as follows:

```
~]# systemctl mask <service>
```

To unmask, execute the following:

```
~]# systemctl unmask <service>
```

When modifying service unit files (and this is not limited to services only), it is best practice to copy the original service file, which is located at `/lib/systemd/system` to `/etc/systemd/service`. Alternatively, you can create a directory in `/etc/systemd/service` appended with `.d`, in which you will create `conf` files containing only the directives that you wish to add or change, as in the previous recipe. The advantage of the latter is that you don't need to keep up with changes in the original service file as it will be "updated" with whatever is located in the `service.d` directory.

See also

For more information about managing `systemd` services, go to `https://access.redhat.com/documentation/en-US/Red_Hat_Enterprise_Linux/7/html/System_Administrators_Guide/sect-Managing_Services_with_systemd-Services.html`.

Configuring the systemd journal for persistence

By default, the journal doesn't store log files on disk, only in memory or the `/run/log/journal` directory. This is sufficient for the recent log history (with the journal) but not for long-term log retention should you decide to go with journal only and not with any other `syslog` solution.

How to do it...

Configuring `journald` to keep more logs than memory allows is fairly simple, as follows:

1. Open `/etc/systemd/journald.conf` with your favorite text editor with root permissions by executing the following command:

   ```
   ~]# vim /etc/systemd/journald.conf
   ```

2. Ensure that the line containing `Storage` is either remarked or set to `auto` or `persistent` and save it, as follows:

   ```
   Storage=auto
   ```

3. If you select `auto`, the journal directory needs to be manually created. The following command would be useful for this:

   ```
   ~]# mkdir -p /var/log/journal
   ```

4. Now, restart the journal service by executing the following command:

   ```
   ~]# systemctl restart systemd-journald
   ```

There's more...

There are many other options that can be set for the journal daemon.

By default, all the data stored by `journald` is compressed, but you could disable this using `Compress=no`.

It is recommended to limit the size of the journal files by either specifying a maximum retention age (`MaxRetentionSec`), a global maximum size usage (`SystemMaxUse`), or a maximum size usage per file (`SystemMaxFileSize`).

See also

For more information about using the journal with RHEL 7, go to `https://access.redhat.com/documentation/en-US/Red_Hat_Enterprise_Linux/7/html/System_Administrators_Guide/s1-Using_the_Journal.html`.

Take a look at the man page for *journald (5)* for more information on what can be configured.

Monitoring services using journalctl

Systemd's journal has the added advantage that its controls allow you to easily narrow down on messages generated by specific services.

How to do it...

Here are the steps you need to perform for this recipe:

1. First, display all the messages generated by your system.

   This will show all the messages generated on the system; run the following commands:

   ```
   ~]# journalctl
   -- Logs begin at Fri 2015-06-26 23:37:30 CEST, end at Sat 2015-07-
   25 00:30:01 CEST. --
   Jun 26 23:37:30 rhel7.mydomain.lan systemd-journal[106]: Runtime
   journal is using 8.0M (max 396.0M, leaving 594.0M of free 3.8G,
   current limit 396.0M).
   Jun 26 23:37:30 rhel7.mydomain.lan systemd-journal[106]: Runtime
   journal is using 8.0M (max 396.0M, leaving 594.0M of free 3.8G,
   current limit 396.0M).
   Jun 26 23:37:30 rhel7.mydomain.lan kernel: Initializing cgroup
   subsys cpuset

   ...
   ~]#
   ```

2. Now, display all system-related messages.

   This command shows all the messages related to the system and not its users:

   ```
   ~]# journalctl --system
   -- Logs begin at Fri 2015-06-26 23:37:30 CEST, end at Sat 2015-07-
   25 00:30:01 CEST. --
   Jun 26 23:37:30 rhel7.mydomain.lan systemd-journal[106]: Runtime
   journal is using 8.0M (max 396.0M, leaving 594.0M of free 3.8G,
   current limit 396.0M).
   Jun 26 23:37:30 rhel7.mydomain.lan systemd-journal[106]: Runtime
   journal is using 8.0M (max 396.0M, leaving 594.0M of free 3.8G,
   current limit 396.0M).
   Jun 26 23:37:30 rhel7.mydomain.lan kernel: Initializing cgroup
   subsys cpuset

   ...
   ~]#
   ```

3. Display all the current user messages.

   This command shows all messages related to the user that you are logged on with:

   ```
   ~]# journalctl --user

   No journal files were found.

   ~]#
   ```

4. Next, display all messages generated by a particular service using the following command line:

   ```
   ~]# journalctl --unit=<service>
   ```

   Here's an example:

   ```
   ~]# journalctl --unit=sshd
   -- Logs begin at Fri 2015-06-26 23:37:30 CEST, end at Sat 2015-07-
   25 00:45:01 CEST. --
   Jun 26 23:40:18 rhel7.mydomain.lan systemd[1]: Starting OpenSSH
   server daemon...
   Jun 26 23:40:18 rhel7.mydomain.lan systemd[1]: Started OpenSSH
   server daemon.
   Jun 26 23:40:20 rhel7.mydomain.lan sshd[817]: Server listening on
   0.0.0.0 port 22.
   Jun 26 23:40:20 rhel7.mydomain.lan sshd[817]: Server listening on
   :: port 22.
   Jun 27 11:30:08 rhel7.mydomain.lan sshd[4495]: Accepted publickey
   for root from 10.0.0.2 port 42748 ssh2: RSA cf:8a:a0:b4:4c:3d:d7:4
   d:93:c6:e0:fe:c0:66:e4
   ...
   ~]#
   ```

5. Now, display messages by priority.

   Priorities can be specified by a keyword or number, such as debug (7), info (6), notice (5), warning (4), err (3), crit (2), alert (1), and emerg (0). When specifying a priority, this includes all the lower priorities as well. For example, err implies that crit, alert, and emerg are also shown. Take a look at the following command line:

   ```
   ~]# journalctl -p <priority>
   ```

   Here's an example:

   ```
   ~]# journalctl -p err
   -- Logs begin at Fri 2015-06-26 23:37:30 CEST, end at Fri 2015-07-
   24 22:30:01 CEST. --
   Jun 26 23:37:30 rhel7.mydomain.lan kernel: ioremap error for
   0xdffff000-0xe0000000, requested 0x10, got 0x0
   ```

```
Jun 26 23:38:49 rhel7.mydomain.lan systemd[1]: Failed unmounting /
usr.

...

~]#
```

6. Next, display messages by time.

You can show all messages from the current boot through the following commands:

```
~]# journalctl -b
-- Logs begin at Fri 2015-06-26 23:37:30 CEST, end at Sat 2015-07-
25 00:45:01 CEST. --
Jun 26 23:37:30 rhel7.mydomain.lan systemd-journal[106]: Runtime
journal is using 8.0M (max 396.0M, leaving 594.0M of free 3.8G,
current limit 396.0M).
Jun 26 23:37:30 rhel7.mydomain.lan systemd-journal[106]: Runtime
journal is using 8.0M (max 396.0M, leaving 594.0M of free 3.8G,
current limit 396.0M).
Jun 26 23:37:30 rhel7.mydomain.lan kernel: Initializing cgroup
subsys cpuset
Jun 26 23:37:30 rhel7.mydomain.lan kernel: Initializing cgroup
subsys cpu
Jun 26 23:37:30 rhel7.mydomain.lan kernel: Initializing cgroup
subsys cpuacct
Jun 26 23:37:30 rhel7.mydomain.lan kernel: Linux version 3.10.0-
229.4.2.el7.x86_64 (gcc version 4.8.2 20140120 (Red Hat 4.8.2-
Jun 26 23:37:30 rhel7.mydomain.lan kernel: Command line: BOOT_
IMAGE=/vmlinuz-3.10.0-229.4.2.el7.x86_64 root=/dev/mapper/rhel7_
system-root ro vconsole.keymap=
Jun 26 23:37:30 rhel7.mydomain.lan kernel: e820: BIOS-provided
physical RAM map:
~]#
```

You can even show all the messages within a specific time range by running the following:

```
~]# journalctl --since="2015-07-24 08:00:00" --until="2015-07-24
09:00:00"
-- Logs begin at Fri 2015-06-26 23:37:30 CEST, end at Sat 2015-07-
25 00:45:01 CEST. --
Jul 24 08:00:01 rhel7.mydomain.lan systemd[1]: Created slice user-
48.slice.
Jul 24 08:00:01 rhel7.mydomain.lan systemd[1]: Starting Session
3331 of user apache.
J
```

```
. . .
Jul 24 08:45:01 rhel7.mydomain.lan systemd[1]: Starting Session
3335 of user apache.
Jul 24 08:45:01 rhel7.mydomain.lan systemd[1]: Started Session
3335 of user apache.
Jul 24 08:45:01 rhel7.mydomain.lan CROND[22909]: (apache) CMD (php
-f /var/lib/owncloud/cron.php)
~]#
```

There's more...

The examples presented in this recipe can all be combined. For instance, if you want to show all the error messages between 8:00 and 9:00 on 2015-07-24, your command would be the following:

```
~]# journalctl -p err --since="2015-07-24 08:00:00" --until="2015-07-24
09:00:00"
```

A lot of people tend to "follow" log files to determine what is happening, hoping to figure out any issues. The `journalctl` binary is an executable one, so it is impossible to use the traditional "following" techniques such as `tail -f` or using `less` and pressing *CTRL + F*. The good folks that coded `systemd` and `systemctl` have provided a solution to this: simply add `-f` or `--follow` as an argument to the `journalctl` command.

Although most environments are used to create `syslog` messages to troubleshoot, the journal does provide the added value of being able to create simple filters that allow you to monitor their messages live.

See also

For more information about using the journal with RHEL 7, go to `https://access.redhat.com/documentation/en-US/Red_Hat_Enterprise_Linux/7/html/System_Administrators_Guide/s1-Using_the_Journal.html`.

Take a look at the man page of *journalctl (1)* for more information on what can be configured.

Configuring logrotate

The `logrotate` tool allows you to rotate the logs that are generated by applications and scripts

It keeps your log directories clutter-free and minimizes disk usage when correctly configured.

How to do it...

The `logrotate` tool is installed by default, but I will include the installation instructions here for completeness. This recipe will show you how to rotate logs for `rsyslog`. We will rotate the logs everyday, add an extension based on the date, compress them with a one-day delay, and keep them for 365 days. Perform the following steps:

1. First, to install `logrotate`, perform the following command:

    ```
    ~]# yum install -y logrotate
    ```

2. Ensure that it's enabled through the following:

    ```
    ~]# systemctl restart crond
    ```

3. Open `/etc/logrotate.d/syslog` with your favorite editor. The contents of this file are the following, by default:

    ```
    /var/log/cron
    /var/log/maillog
    /var/log/messages
    /var/log/secure
    /var/log/spooler
    {
        sharedscripts
        postrotate
            /bin/kill -HUP `cat /var/run/syslogd.pid 2>
    /dev/null` 2> /dev/null || true
        endscript
    }
    ```

4. Now, replace this with the following code:

    ```
    /var/log/cron
    /var/log/maillog
    /var/log/messages
    /var/log/secure
    /var/log/spooler
    {
        compress
        daily
        delaycompress
        dateext
        missingok
        rotate 365
        sharedscripts
        postrotate
    ```

```
            /bin/kill -HUP `cat /var/run/syslogd.pid 2>
    /dev/null` 2> /dev/null || true
        endscript
    }
```

5. Finally, save the file.

How it works...

The `logrotate` tool is a script that is launched by cron everyday.

The directives added to the default `logrotate` definition are `compress`, `daily`, `delaycompress`, `dateext`, `missingok`, and `rotate`.

The `compress` directive compresses old versions of the log files with gzip. This behavior is somewhat changed by specifying `delaycompress`. This causes us to always have the most recently rotated log file available uncompressed.

The `daily` directive makes `logrotate` execute the definition every day. The `rotate` directive only keeps x rotated log files before deleting the oldest. In this case, we have specified this to be 365, which means that while rotating daily, the logs are kept for 365 days.

The `missingok` directive makes it alright for `syslog` to not create a file, which, however unlikely, is possible.

The `dateext` directive appends a date to the rotated file in the form of `yyyymmdd` instead of a number, which is the default.

There's more...

The `/etc/logrotate.conf` file contains the defaults directives for all definitions. If you don't specifically use a directive within a definition for a file, the values in this file will be used if specified.

It would make sense to change the settings in this file so that all the definitions are affected, but this is not practical; not all log files are made equal. The `syslog` service generates a lot of messages, and it would probably clutter up your system before long. However, yum, for instance, doesn't generate a lot of messages, and it keeps this log file readable for much longer than your `syslog` files. This, by the way, is reflected in the definition for yum.

If you want to debug your new configuration, this can be achieved by executing the following to test just one configuration:

```
~# /usr/sbin/logrotate -v /etc/logrotate.d/<config file>
```

Alternatively, you can use the following to test everything:

```
~]# /usr/sbin/logrotate -v /etc/logrotate.conf
```

Here's an example:

```
~]# /usr/sbin/logrotate -v /etc/logrotate.d/syslog
reading config file /etc/logrotate.d/syslog

Handling 1 logs

rotating pattern: /var/log/cron
/var/log/maillog
/var/log/messages
/var/log/secure
/var/log/spooler
 1048576 bytes (no old logs will be kept)
empty log files are rotated, old logs are removed
considering log /var/log/cron
  log does not need rotating
considering log /var/log/maillog
  log does not need rotating
considering log /var/log/messages
  log does not need rotating
considering log /var/log/secure
  log does not need rotating
considering log /var/log/spooler
  log does not need rotating
not running postrotate script, since no logs were rotated
~]#
```

See also

Take a look at the man page of *logrotate (8)* for more information on configuring `logrotate`.

Managing time

RHEL 7 comes preinstalled with Chrony. While everybody knows Ntpd, Chrony is a newcomer to the game of timekeeping.

Chrony is a set of programs that maintains the time on your computer using different time sources, such as NTP servers, your system's clock, and even custom-made scripts/programs. It also calculates the rate at which the computer loses or gains time to compensate while no external reference is present—for example, if your NTP server(s) is(are) down.

Chrony is a good solution for systems which are intermittently disconnected and reconnected to a network.

Ntpd should be considered for systems that are normally kept on permanently.

How to do it...

When talking about managing time in RHEL, it can be done through:

▶ Chrony

▶ Ntpd

We'll take a look at each of the methods separately.

Managing time through chrony

Ensure that chrony is installed and enabled, and perform the following steps:

1. First, install chrony through the following command:

    ```
    ~]# yum install -y chrony
    ```

2. Enable chrony, as follows:

    ```
    ~]# systemctl enable chrony
    ~]# systemctl start chrony
    ```

3. Now, open /etc/chrony.conf with your favorite editor and look for lines starting with the server directive using the following commands:

    ```
    server 0.rhel.pool.ntp.org iburst
    server 1.rhel.pool.ntp.org iburst
    server 2.rhel.pool.ntp.org iburst
    server 3.rhel.pool.ntp.org iburst
    ```

4. Next, replace these lines with NTP servers that are near you and save the file:

```
server 0.pool.ntp.mydomain.lan iburst
server 1.pool.ntp.mydomain.lan iburst
```

   The `iburst` option causes NTP to send a burst of eight packets at the next poll instead of just one if the time master is unavailable, causing the NTP daemon to speed up time synchronization.

5. Finally, restart `chrony` by executing the following command:

```
~]# systemctl restart chrony
```

Managing time through ntpd

Ensure that `ntpd` is installed and enabled, and perform the following steps:

1. First, install `ntpd` by running the following:

```
~]# yum install -y ntpd
```

2. Enable `ntpd` through this command:

```
~]# systemctl enable ntpd
```

3. Open `/etc/ntp.conf` with your favorite editor and look for the lines starting with the `server` directive. Run the following:

```
server 0.rhel.pool.ntp.org iburst
server 1.rhel.pool.ntp.org iburst
server 2.rhel.pool.ntp.org iburst
server 3.rhel.pool.ntp.org iburst
```

4. Replace these lines with the NTP servers near you and save the file:

```
server 0.pool.ntp.mydomain.lan iburst
server 1.pool.ntp.mydomain.lan iburst
```

5. Replace the contents of `/etc/ntp/step-tickers` with all your NTP servers, one per line:

```
0.pool.ntp.mydomain.lan
1.pool.ntp.mydomain.lan
```

6. Now, restart `ntpd` by executing the following:

```
~]# systemctl restart ntpd
```

There's more...

While `ntpd` is the obvious choice for time synchronization, it doesn't fare well in environments where time masters are intermittently accessible (for whatever reason). In these environments, `chronyd` thrives. Also, `ntpd` can be quite complex to configure correctly, whereas `chronyd` is a little bit simpler.

The reason for modifying `/etc/ntp/step-tickers` when using the `ntpd` file is for the startup of the service. It uses `ntpdate` to synchronize time in one step before actually starting the NTP daemon itself, which is a lot slower in synchronizing time.

To figure out whether your system is synchronized, use the following command:

 ▶ For `chrony`, use the following command:

 `~]# chronyc sources`

 ▶ For `ntpd`, run the following:

 `~]# ntpq -p`

Your output will be similar to:

```
remote          refid       st t when poll reach   delay   offset  jitter
==============================================================================
 LOCAL(0)       .LOCL.       5 1  60m   64    0    0.000    0.000   0.000
*master.exam 178.32.44.208  3 u   35  128  377    0.214   -0.651  14.285
```

The asterisk (*) in front of an entry means that your system is synchronized to this remote system's clock.

See also

For more information on configuring `chrony` for RHEL 7, go to `https://access.redhat.com/documentation/en-US/Red_Hat_Enterprise_Linux/7/html/System_Administrators_Guide/ch-Configuring_NTP_Using_the_chrony_Suite.html`.

For more information on configuring `ntpd` for RHEL 7, go to `https://access.redhat.com/documentation/en-US/Red_Hat_Enterprise_Linux/7/html/System_Administrators_Guide/ch-Configuring_NTP_Using_ntpd.html`.

Configuring your boot environment

GRUB2 is the default boot loader for RHEL 7. By default, it doesn't use any fancy configuration options, but it is wise to at least secure your grub boot loader.

How to do it...

There are many advantages to having your grub and boot environment output to serial console in an enterprise environment. Many vendors integrate virtual serial ports in their remote control systems, as does KVM. This allows you to connect to the serial port and easily grab whatever is displayed in a text editor.

Setting a password on the GRUB2 boot loader mitigates possible hacking attempts on your system when you have physical access to the server or console. Perform the following steps for this recipe:

1. First, edit `/etc/sysconfig/grub` with your favorite editor.

2. Now, modify the `GRUB_TERMINAL_OUTPUT` line to include both console and serial access by executing the following command line:

   ```
   GRUB_TERMINAL_OUTPUT="console serial"
   ```

3. Add the `GRUB_SERIAL_COMMAND` entry, as follows:

   ```
   GRUB_SERIAL_COMMAND="serial --speed=9600 --unit=0 --word=8
   --parity=no -stop=1"
   ```

4. Now, save the file.

5. Create the `/etc/grub.d/01_users` file with the following contents:

   ```
   cat << EOF
   set superusers="root"
   password root SuperSecretPassword
   EOF
   ```

6. Next, update your `grub` configuration by running the following commands:

   ```
   ~]# grub2-mkconfig -o /boot/grub2/grub.cfg
   Generating grub configuration file ...
   Found linux image: /boot/vmlinuz-3.10.0-229.4.2.el7.x86_64
   Found initrd image: /boot/initramfs-3.10.0-229.4.2.el7.x86_64.img
   Found linux image: /boot/vmlinuz-3.10.0-229.1.2.el7.x86_64
   Found initrd image: /boot/initramfs-3.10.0-229.1.2.el7.x86_64.img
   Found linux image: /boot/vmlinuz-0-rescue-fe045089e49942cb97db6758
   92395bc8
   Found initrd image: /boot/initramfs-0-rescue-fe045089e49942cb97db6
   75892395bc8.img
   done
   ~]#
   ```

How it works...

The behavior of `grub2-mkconfig` is defined by the directives of the files in `/etc/grub.d`. These files, based on the configuration in `/etc/sysconfig/grub`, autogenerate all the menu entries in the `grub.cfg` file. You can modify its behavior by adding files with bash code in this directory.

For instance, you could add a script that would add a menu entry to boot from the CD/DVD ROM drive.

The user root, which is added to `/etc/grub.d/01_users`, is the only one allowed to edit menu entries from the console, mitigating the weakness in GRUB to force rescue mode by adding `1` or `rescue` at the end of the `kernel` line.

There's more...

The `grub2-mkconfig` command is specific for BIOS-based systems. In order to do the same on UEFI systems, modify the command as follows:

```
~]# grub2-mkconfig -o /boot/efi/EFI/redhat/grub.cfg
```

In order to access the GRUB terminal over the same serial connection, you need to specify an additional kernel option: `console=ttyS0,9600n8`.

You can either modify the kernel lines in `/boot/grub2/grub.cfg` (or `/boot/efi/EFI/redhat/grub.cfg` manually, but you do risk losing the change when your kernel is updated), or manually regenerate the file using `grub2-mkconfig`.

It's best to add it to the `GRUB_CMDLINE_LINUX` directive in `/etc/sysconfig/grub` and regenerate your `grub.cfg` file.

Passwords for GRUB users can be encrypted using the `grub2-mkpasswd-pbkdf2` command, as follows:

```
~]# grub2-mkpasswd-pbkdf2
Enter password:
Reenter password:
PBKDF2 hash of your password is grub.pbkdf2.sha512.10000.C208DD5E318B1D64
77C4E51035649C197411259C214D0B83E3E83753AD58F7676B62CDF48E31AF0E739844A5
CF9A95F76AF5008AF340336DB50ECA23906ECC13.9D20A66F0CADA12AA617B293B5BBF7
AAD44423ECA513F302FEBF5CB92A0DC54436E16D7CD6E09685323084A27462C2A981054
D52F452F5C2F71FBACD2C31AEFA
~]#
```

Then, you can substitute the clear text password in `/etc/grub.d/01_users` with the generated hash. Here's an example:

```
password root
grub.pbkdf2.sha512.10000.C208DD5E318B1D6477C4E51035649C197411259C2
14D0B83E3E83753AD58F7676B62CDF48E31AF0E739844A5CF9A95F76AF5008AF34
0336DB50ECA23906ECC13.9D20A66F0CADA12AA617B293B5BBF7AAD44423ECA513
F302FEBF5CB92A0DC54436E16D7CD6E09685323084A27462C2A981054D52F452F5
C2F71FBACD2C31AEFA
```

All the entries that are automatically generated are bootable but not editable from the console, unless you know the user and password. If you have custom menu entries and want to protect them in a similar way, add `--unrestricted` to the menu entry definition before the accolades. Here's an example:

```
menuentry 'My custom grub boot entry' <options> --unrestricted {
```

See also

For more information about working with the GRUB2 boot loader, go to `https://access.redhat.com/documentation/en-US/Red_Hat_Enterprise_Linux/7/html/System_Administrators_Guide/ch-Working_with_the_GRUB_2_Boot_Loader.html`.

Configuring smtp

Many programs use (or can be configured to use) SMTP to send messages about their status and so on. By default, postfix is configured to deliver all messages locally and not respond to incoming mails. If you have an environment of multiple servers, this can become quite tedious to log on to each server to check for new mail. This recipe will show you how to relay messages to a central mail relay or message store that also uses SMTP.

Postfix is installed by default on RHEL 7.

How to do it...

In this recipe, we'll combine several options:

- We'll allow the server to accept incoming mails
- We'll only allow the server to relay messages from recipients in the `mydomain.lan` domain
- We'll forward all mails to the `mailhost.mydomain.lan` mailserver

To complete this recipe, perform the following steps:

1. Edit `/etc/postfix/main.cf` with your favorite editor.

2. Modify `inet_interface` to accept mails on any interface through the following command:

   ```
   inet_interface = all
   ```

3. Add the `smtpd_recipient_restrictions` directive to only allow incoming mails from the `mydomain.lan` domain, as follows:

   ```
   smtpd_recipient_restrictions =
       check_sender_access hash:/etc/postfix/sender_access,
       reject
   ```

   As you can see, the last two lines are indented. The `postfix` considers this block as one line instead of three separate lines.

4. Add the `relayhost` directive to point to `mailhost.mydomain.lan`, as follows:

   ```
   relayhost = mailhost.mydomain.lan
   ```

5. Now, save the `postfix` file.

6. Create `/etc/postfix/sender_access` with the following contents:

   ```
   mydomain.lan OK
   ```

7. Next, hash the `/etc/postfix/access` file using the following command:

   ```
   ~]# postmap /etc/postfix/access
   ```

8. Finally, restart `postfix`, as follows:

   ```
   ~]# systemctl restart postfix
   ```

There's more...

To monitor your mail queue on the system, execute the following:

```
~]# postqueue -p
```

Whenever your mail relay cannot forward mails, it stores them locally and tries to resend them at a later time. When you restore the mailflow, you can flush the queue and attempt delivery by executing the following:

```
~]# postqueue -f
```

The kind of setup presented in this recipe is quite simple and assumes that you don't have malicious users on your network. There are software that allow you to mitigate spam and viruses. Popular solutions for this are `spamassassin` and `amavis`.

See also

For more information on using postfix with RHEL 7, go to `https://access.redhat.com/documentation/en-US/Red_Hat_Enterprise_Linux/7/html/System_Administrators_Guide/s1-email-mta.html#s2-email-mta-postfix`.

For more information on postfix, check out the postfix rpm (`rpm -ql postfix`) or go to `http://www.postfix.org/`. This site provides good documentation and *how to*'s for a large number of scenarios.

5
Using SELinux

Here is an overview of the recipes presented in this chapter:

- ▸ Changing file contexts
- ▸ Configuring SELinux booleans
- ▸ Configuring SELinux port definitions
- ▸ Troubleshooting SELinux
- ▸ Creating SELinux policies
- ▸ Applying SELinux policies

Introduction

SELinux is a Linux kernel module that allows supporting **mandatory access control** (MAC) security policies. The Red Hat implementation of SELinux combines **role-based access control** (**RBAC**) with **type enforcement** (**TE**). Optionally, **multilevel security** (**MLS**) is also available but isn't widely used as it implements fewer policies than the default Red Hat SELinux policies.

SELinux is enabled by default in RHEL 7 and supported for all software packaged by Red Hat.

The recipes presented in this chapter will not only provide you with a solid base to troubleshoot SELinux issues and fix them, but also a peek into how to create your own SELinux policies.

Changing file contexts

Files and processes are labeled with a SELinux context, which contains additional information about a SELinux user, role type, and level. This information is provided by the SELinux kernel module to make access control decisions.

The SELinux user, a unique identity known by the SELinux policy, is authorized for a number of roles.

SELinux roles, as we already alluded to before, are attributes of SELinux users and part of the RBAC SELinux policy. SELinux roles are authorized for SELinux domains.

SELinux types define the type for files and domain for processes. SELinux policies define access between types and other files and processes. By default, if there is no specific rule in the SELinux policy, access is denied.

The SELinux level is only used when the SELinux type is set to MLS and should be avoided altogether on anything other than servers. This set of policies doesn't cover the same domains as defined by the default Red Hat SELinux policy. The SELinux level is an attribute of MLS and **multi-category security (MCS)**.

Getting ready

All files and processes on a system are labeled to represent security-relevant information. This information is called the SELinux context. To view the contexts of files (and directories), execute the following:

```
~# ls -Z
-rw-r--r--. root root unconfined_u:object_r:admin_home_t:s0 file
~#
```

How to do it...

You can temporarily change the context of a file (or files) or permanently change their context. The first option allows easy troubleshooting if you need to figure out whether changing the context solves your problem. Persistent changes are mostly used when your applications refer to data that is not in the standard location—for example, if your web server serves data from `/srv/www`.

Temporary context changes

Temporary SELinux context changes remain until the file, or the filesystem that the file resides on, is relabeled.

To change the SELinux user of a file, execute the following:

```
~# chcon --user <SELinux user> <filename>
```

To change the SELinux role of a file, execute the following:

```
~# chcon --role <SELinux role> <filename>
```

To change the SELinux type of a file, execute the following:

```
~# chcon --type <SELinux typs> <filename>
```

Persistent file context changes

Changing the application data location doesn't automatically modify SELinux contexts to allow your application to access this data.

To permanently relabel files or directories, perform the following:

1. Change the SELinux user for your files or directories via this command:

   ```
   ~# semanage fcontext -a --seuser <SELinux user> <filename|dirname>
   ```

2. Change the SELinux type of your files or directories by running the following:

   ```
   ~# semanage fcontext -a --type <SELinux type> <filename|dirname>
   ```

3. Finish with this command line by applying the directive to the `files/directories`:

   ```
   ~# restorecon <filename|dirname>
   ```

There's more...

To show all the available SELinux users, execute the following:

```
~# semanage user -l
```

```
~]# semanage user -l

                Labeling   MLS/        MLS/
SELinux User    Prefix     MCS Level   MCS Range                SELinux Roles

guest_u         user       s0          s0                       guest_r
root            user       s0          s0-s0:c0.c1023           staff_r sysadm_r system_r unconfined_r
staff_u         user       s0          s0-s0:c0.c1023           staff_r sysadm_r system_r unconfined_r
sysadm_u        user       s0          s0-s0:c0.c1023           sysadm_r
system_u        user       s0          s0-s0:c0.c1023           system_r unconfined_r
unconfined_u    user       s0          s0-s0:c0.c1023           system_r unconfined_r
user_u          user       s0          s0                       user_r
xguest_u        user       s0          s0                       xguest_r
~]# []
```

Alternatively, you can install the `setools-console` package and run the following:

```
~# seinfo -u
```

```
~]# seinfo -u

Users: 8
   sysadm_u
   system_u
   xguest_u
   root
   guest_u
   staff_u
   user_u
   unconfined_u
~]# 
```

To show all the available SELinux types, install the `setools-console` package and run the following:

```
~# seinfo -t
```

```
~]# seinfo -t

Types: 4624
    bluetooth_conf_t
    cmirrord_exec_t
    colord_exec_t
    foghorn_exec_t
    jacorb_port_t
    pki_ra_exec_t
    pki_ra_lock_t
    sosreport_t
    squid_script_exec_t
    etc_runtime_t
    fenced_tmp_t
    git_session_t
    glance_port_t
    osad_log_t
    presence_port_t
    samba_secrets_t
    snort_exec_t
    sshd_sandbox_t
    audisp_var_run_t
    auditd_var_run_t
    blktap_var_run_t
    cfengine_execd_t
    cinder_var_lib_t
    cinder_var_run_t
    colord_var_lib_t
    comsat_var_run_t
    condor_var_lib_t
    condor_var_run_t
    conman_var_run_t
```

To show the available SELinux roles, install the `setools-console` package and run the following:

```
~# seinfo -r
```

```
~]# seinfo -r

Roles: 14
    auditadm_r
    dbadm_r
    guest_r
    staff_r
    user_r
    logadm_r
    object_r
    secadm_r
    sysadm_r
    system_r
    webadm_r
    xguest_r
    nx_server_r
    unconfined_r
~]# []
```

The `semanage` tool doesn't have an option to include all files recursively, but there is a solution to this. The filename or dirname you specify is actually a regular expression filter. So, for example, if you want to recursively include all the files in `/srv/www`, you could specify "`/srv/www(/.*)?`".

> For now, there's no way to change the SELinux role using `semanage`.
> A way to get around this is to change the SELinux user or type using
> `semanage` and then edit it, as follows: `/etc/selinux/targeted/contexts/files/file_contexts.local`.

Here's a wrong SELinux context example of an AVC denial report found in the `audit.log` file:

```
type=AVC msg=audit(1438884962.645:86): avc:  denied  { open } for
pid=1283 comm="httpd" path="/var/www/html/index.html" dev="dm-5"
ino=1089 scontext=system_u:system_r:httpd_t:s0
tcontext=system_u:object_r:user_home_t:s0 tclass=file
```

This command can be explained as follows:

Commands	Description
`type=AVC`	This is the log type
`msg=audit(1438884962.645:86)`	This is the log entry timestamp
`avc`	This is a repetition of the log type
`denied`	This states whether enforcing is enabled
`{ open }`	This is a permission that causes AVC denial
`for  pid=1283`	This is the process ID
`comm="httpd"`	This is the process command
`path="/var/www/html/index.html"`	This is the path that is accessed
`dev="dm-5"`	This blocks the device that the preceding file is located on
`ino=1089`	This is the inode of the preceding file
`scontext=system_u:system_r:httpd_t:s0`	This is the source SELinux context
`tcontext=system_u:object_r:user_home_t:s0`	This is the target SELinux context
`tclass=file`	This is the target SELinux class

See also

Refer to the man page for *chcon (1)* and *semanage-fcontext (8)* for more information.

Configuring SELinux booleans

SELinux booleans allow you to change the SELinux policy at runtime without the need to write additional policies. This allows you to change the policy without the need for recompilation, such as allowing services to access NFS volumes.

How to do it...

This is the way to temporarily or permanently change SELinux booleans.

Listing SELinux booleans

For a list of all booleans and an explanation of what they do, execute the following:

```
~# semanage boolean -l
```

Now, let's try to get the value of a particular SELinux boolean. It is possible to get the value of a single SELinux boolean without the use of additional utilities, such as **grep** and/or **awk**. Simply execute the following:

```
~# getsebool <SELinux boolean>
```

This shows you whether or not the boolean is set. Here's an example:

```
~# getsebool virt_use_nfs

virt_use_nfs --> off

~#
```

Changing SELinux booleans

To set a boolean value to a particular one, use the following command:

```
~# setsebool <SELinux boolean> <on|off>
```

Here's an example command:

```
~# setsebool virt_use_nfs on
```

This command allows you to change the value of the boolean, but it is not persistent across reboots. To allow persistence, add the -P option to the command line, as follows:

```
~# setsebool -P virt_use_nfs on
```

There's more...

If you would like a list of all the bare bones of SELinux booleans and their values, getsebool -a is an alternative, as follows:

```
~# getsebool -a
```

```
~]# getsebool -a | head -n32
abrt_anon_write --> off
abrt_handle_event --> off
abrt_upload_watch_anon_write --> on
antivirus_can_scan_system --> off
antivirus_use_jit --> off
auditadm_exec_content --> on
authlogin_nsswitch_use_ldap --> off
authlogin_radius --> off
authlogin_yubikey --> off
awstats_purge_apache_log_files --> off
boinc_execmem --> on
cdrecord_read_content --> off
cluster_can_network_connect --> off
cluster_manage_all_files --> off
cluster_use_execmem --> off
cobbler_anon_write --> off
cobbler_can_network_connect --> off
cobbler_use_cifs --> off
cobbler_use_nfs --> off
collectd_tcp_network_connect --> off
condor_tcp_network_connect --> off
conman_can_network --> off
cron_can_relabel --> off
cron_system_cronjob_use_shares --> off
cron_userdomain_transition --> on
cups_execmem --> off
cvs_read_shadow --> off
daemons_dump_core --> off
daemons_enable_cluster_mode --> off
daemons_use_tcp_wrapper --> off
daemons_use_tty --> off
```

Managing SELinux booleans can be rather complex as there are a lot of booleans, and their names are not always simple to remember. For this reason, the `setsebool`, `getsebool`, and `semanage` tools come with tab completion. So, whenever you type any boolean name, you can use the `tab` key to complete or display the possible options.

Here's an example of an AVC denial report found in the `audit.log` file that can be solved by enabling a boolean:

```
type=AVC msg=audit(1438884483.053:48): avc:  denied  { open } for
pid=1270 comm="httpd" path="/nfs/www/html/index.html" dev="0:38"
ino=2717909250 scontext=system_u:system_r:httpd_t:s0
tcontext=system_u:object_r:nfs_t:s0 tclass=file
```

This is an example of a service (`httpd` in this case) accessing a file located on an NFS share, which is disabled by default.

This can be allowed by setting the `httpd_use_nfs` boolean to "on".

Configuring SELinux port definitions

SELinux also controls access to your TCP/IP ports. If your application is confined by SELinux, it will also deny access to your ports when starting up the application.

This recipe will show you how to detect which ports are used by a particular SELinux type and change it.

How to do it...

Let's allow the HTTP daemon to listen on the nonstandard port `82` through the following steps:

1. First, look for the ports that are accessed by HTTP via these commands:

```
~# semanage port -l |grep http
http_cache_port_t               tcp      8080, 8118, 8123, 10001-
10010
http_cache_port_t               udp      3130
http_port_t                     tcp      80, 81, 443, 488, 8008,
8009, 8443, 9000
pegasus_http_port_t             tcp      5988
pegasus_https_port_t            tcp      5989
~#
```

The SELinux port assignment we're looking for is `http_port_t`. As you can see, only the displayed ports (80, 81, 443, 488, 8008, 8009, 8443, and 9000) are allowed to be used to listen on by any process that is allowed to use the `http_port_t` type.

2. Add port `82` to the list of allowed ports, as follows:

```
~# semanage port -a -t http_port_t -p tcp 82
~#
```

3. Next, verify the port assignment, as follows:

```
~# semanage port -l |grep ^http_port_t
http_port_t                    tcp        82, 80, 81, 443, 488,
8008, 8009, 8443, 9000
~#
```

There's more...

In this example, there is reference to the HTTP daemon as the SELinux policy governing HTTP daemons is implemented not only for the Apache web server, but also for Nginx. So, as long as you use the packages provided by Red Hat, the SELinux policies will be used correctly.

Take a look at the following example of an AVC denial report found in the `audit.log` file that is caused because the domain is not allowed to access a certain port:

```
type=AVC msg=audit(1225948455.061:294): avc: denied { name_bind }
for pid=4997 comm="httpd" src=82
scontext=unconfined_u:system_r:httpd_t:s0
tcontext=system_u:object_r:port_t:s0 tclass=tcp_socket
```

This AVC denial shows that the `httpd` daemon attempted to listen (`name_bind`) on port `82` but was prohibited by SELinux.

Troubleshooting SELinux

Troubleshooting SELinux is not as straightforward as it may seem as at the time of writing this book, there is no integration with SELinux to return SELinux-related events back to the applications. Usually, you will find that access is denied with no further description of it in log files.

Getting ready

Make sure that `setroubleshoot-server` and `setools-console` are installed by executing the following command:

```
~# yum install -y setroubleshoot-server setools-console
```

If you have X server installed on your system, you can also install the GUI, as follows:

```
~# yum install -y setroubleshoot
```

Make sure that `auditd`, `rsyslog`, and `setroubleshootd` are installed and running before reproducing the issue.

How to do it...

There are several ways to detect SELinux issues.

This is a classic issue where the SELinux context of a file is incorrect, causing the application trying to access the file to fail.

In this case, the context of `/var/www/html/index.html` is set to `system_u:object_r:user_home_t:s0` instead of `system_u:object_r:httpd_sys_content_t:s0`, causing `httpd` to throw a `404`. Take a look at the following command:

```
# ls -Z /var/www/html/index.html
-rw-r--r--. apache apache system_u:object_r:user_home_t:s0 /var/www/html/index.html
~#
```

audit.log

Use the following command to look for denied or failed entries in the audit log:

```
~# egrep 'avc.*denied' /var/log/audit/audit.log
ype=AVC msg=audit(1438884962.645:86): avc:  denied  { open } for
pid=1283 comm="httpd" path="/var/www/html/index.html" dev="dm-5" ino=1089
scontext=system_u:system_r:httpd_t:s0 tcontext=system_u:object_r:user_home_t:s0 tclass=file
~#
```

syslog

You can look for SELinux messages in `/var/log/messages` via the following command:

```
~# grep 'SELinux is preventing' /var/log/messages
Aug  6 20:16:03 localhost setroubleshoot: SELinux is preventing /usr/sbin/httpd from read access on the file index.html. For complete SELinux messages., run sealert -l dc544bde-2d7e-4f3f-8826-224d9b0c71f6
Aug 6 20:16:03 localhost python: SELinux is preventing /usr/sbin/httpd from read access on the file index.html.
~#
```

ausearch

Use the audit search tool to find SELinux errors, as follows:

```
~# ausearch -m avc

time->Thu Aug  6 20:16:02 2015

type=SYSCALL msg=audit(1438884962.645:86): arch=c000003e syscall=2
success=yes exit=25 a0=7f1bcfb65670 a1=80000 a2=0 a3=0 items=0 ppid=1186
pid=1283 auid=4294967295 uid=48 gid=48 euid=48 suid=48 fsuid=48 egid=48
sgid=48 fsgid=48 tty=(none) ses=4294967295 comm="httpd" exe="/usr/sbin/
httpd" subj=system_u:system_r:httpd_t:s0 key=(null)

type=AVC msg=audit(1438884962.645:86): avc:  denied  { open } for
pid=1283 comm="httpd" path="/var/www/html/index.html" dev="dm-5" ino=1089
scontext=system_u:system_r:httpd_t:s0 tcontext=system_u:object_r:user_
home_t:s0 tclass=file

type=AVC msg=audit(1438884962.645:86): avc:  denied  { read } for
pid=1283 comm="httpd" name="index.html" dev="dm-5" ino=1089 scontext=s
ystem_u:system_r:httpd_t:s0 tcontext=system_u:object_r:user_home_t:s0
tclass=file

~#
```

Once we restore the context of `/var/www/html/index.html` to its original, the file is accessible again. Take a look at the following commands:

```
~# restorecon /var/www/html/index.html

~# ls -Z /var/www/html/index.html

-rw-r--r--. apache apache system_u:object_r:httpd_sys_content_t:s0 /var/
www/html/index.html

~#
```

There's more...

It's not always easy to determine whether a file has the correct context. To view the actual SELinux context and compare it to what it should be without modifying anything, execute this command:

```
~# matchpathcon -V index.html

index.html has context system_u:object_r:user_home_t:s0, should be
system_u:object_r:httpd_sys_content_t:s0

~#
```

This tells you what the current context is and what it should be.

As you can see in the preceding syslog example, the output comes with the following command:

```
... run sealert -l dc544bde-2d7e-4f3f-8826-224d9b0c71f6
```

This command provides you with a richer description of the problem:

```
~# sealert -l dc544bde-2d7e-4f3f-8826-224d9b0c71f6
SELinux is preventing /usr/sbin/httpd from read access on the file index.
html.


*****  Plugin catchall_boolean (89.3 confidence) suggests
*******************


If you want to allow httpd to read user content
Then you must tell SELinux about this by enabling the 'httpd_read_user_
content' boolean.
You can read 'None' man page for more details.
Do
setsebool -P httpd_read_user_content 1


*****  Plugin catchall (11.6 confidence) suggests
**************************


If you believe that httpd should be allowed read access on the index.html
file by default.
Then you should report this as a bug.
You can generate a local policy module to allow this access.
Do
allow this access for now by executing:
# grep httpd /var/log/audit/audit.log | audit2allow -M mypol
# semodule -i mypol.pp



Additional Information:
Source Context              system_u:system_r:httpd_t:s0
Target Context              system_u:object_r:user_home_t:s0
Target Objects              index.html [ file ]
Source                      httpd
```

Source Path	/usr/sbin/httpd
Port	<Unknown>
Host	localhost.localdomain
Source RPM Packages	httpd-2.4.6-31.el7.rhel.x86_64
Target RPM Packages	
Policy RPM	selinux-policy-3.13.1-23.el7_1.7.noarch
Selinux Enabled	True
Policy Type	targeted
Enforcing Mode	Permissive
Host Name	localhost.localdomain
Platform	Linux localhost.localdomain 3.10.0-229.4.2.el7.x86_64 #1 SMP Wed May 13 10:06:09 UTC 2015 x86_64 x86_64
Alert Count	1
First Seen	2015-08-06 20:16:02 CEST
Last Seen	2015-08-06 20:16:02 CEST
Local ID	dc544bde-2d7e-4f3f-8826-224d9b0c71f6

Raw Audit Messages

```
type=AVC msg=audit(1438884962.645:86): avc:  denied  { read } for
pid=1283 comm="httpd" name="index.html" dev="dm-5" ino=1089 scontext=s
ystem_u:system_r:httpd_t:s0 tcontext=system_u:object_r:user_home_t:s0
tclass=file




type=AVC msg=audit(1438884962.645:86): avc:  denied  { open } for
pid=1283 comm="httpd" path="/var/www/html/index.html" dev="dm-5" ino=1089
scontext=system_u:system_r:httpd_t:s0 tcontext=system_u:object_r:user_
home_t:s0 tclass=file




type=SYSCALL msg=audit(1438884962.645:86): arch=x86_64 syscall=open
success=yes exit=ENOTTY a0=7f1bcfb65670 a1=80000 a2=0 a3=0 items=0
ppid=1186 pid=1283 auid=4294967295 uid=48 gid=48 euid=48 suid=48 fsuid=48
egid=48 sgid=48 fsgid=48 tty=(none) ses=4294967295 comm=httpd exe=/usr/
sbin/httpd subj=system_u:system_r:httpd_t:s0 key=(null)




Hash: httpd,httpd_t,user_home_t,file,read
~#
```

This will actually give you more details about the problem at hand, and it will also make a couple of suggestions. Of course, in this case, the real solution is to restore the SELinux context of the file.

If you have installed a graphical desktop environment, you will get a notification each time your system encounters an "AVC denied" alert:

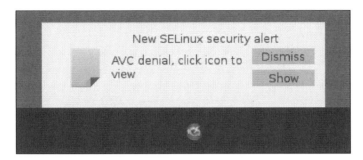

Clicking on the icon will present you with the following dialog:

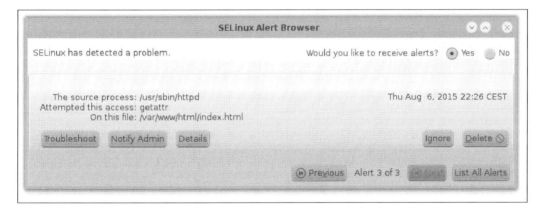

Clicking on the **Troubleshoot** button will provide you with additional information and a (or multiple) possible solution(s) for your problem, as shown in the following screenshot:

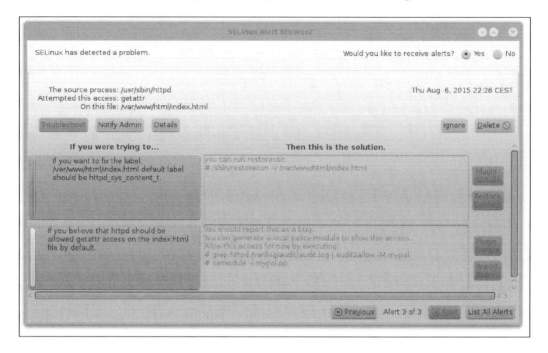

In this case, the first option (the one marked with a green line) is the correct solution.

Some AVC denial messages may not be logged when SELinux denies access. Applications and libraries regularly probe for more access than is actually required to perform their tasks. In order to not flood the audit logs with these kinds of messages, the policy can silence the AVC denials that are without permissions using `dontaudit` rules. The downside of this is that it may make troubleshooting SELinux denials more difficult.

To disable the `dontaudit` rules, execute the following command:

```
~# semanage dontaudit off
```

This will disable the `dontaudit` rules and rebuild the SELinux policy.

It is advisable to reenable the `dontaudit` rules when you're done troubleshooting as this may flood your disks. You can do this by executing the following command:

```
~# semanage dontaudit on
```

To get a full list of `dontaudit` rules, run the following:

```
~# sesearch --dontaudit
Found 8361 semantic av rules:
```

```
dontaudit user_ssh_agent_t user_ssh_agent_t : udp_socket listen ;

dontaudit openshift_user_domain sshd_t : key view ;

dontaudit user_seunshare_t user_seunshare_t : process setfscreate ;

dontaudit ftpd_t selinux_config_t : dir { getattr search open } ;

dontaudit user_seunshare_t user_seunshare_t : capability sys_module ;

dontaudit xguest_dbusd_t xguest_dbusd_t : udp_socket listen ;

dontaudit tuned_t tuned_t : process setfscreate ;

...
~#
```

If you know the domain that you wish to check for `dontaudit` rules, add the `-s` argument followed by the domain, as shown here:

```
~# sesearch --dontaudit -s httpd_t
Found 182 semantic av rules:
    dontaudit httpd_t snmpd_var_lib_t : file { ioctl read write getattr
lock open } ;

    dontaudit domain rpm_var_lib_t : file { ioctl read write getattr lock
append } ;

    dontaudit httpd_t snmpd_var_lib_t : dir { ioctl read getattr lock
search open } ;

    dontaudit domain rpm_var_lib_t : dir getattr ;

    dontaudit httpd_t snmpd_var_lib_t : lnk_file { read getattr } ;

...
~#
```

See also

Take a look at the man page for *ausearch (8)*, *matchpathcon (8)*, and *sealert (8)* for more information.

Creating SELinux policies

In some cases, you'll need to create a new SELinux policy—for instance, when installing a piece of software from source. Although I do not recommend installing software from source on enterprise systems, this is sometimes your only option for company-developed software.

It is then time to create your own SELinux policy.

Getting ready

For this recipe, you need to have `policycoreutils-python` installed.

How to do it...

We'll use the `denied` entries in the `audit.log` log file to build our SELinux policy with `audit2allow`.

In this recipe, we'll use the same example as in the previous recipe: the SELinux context of `/var/www/html/index.html` that is changed to `system_u:object_r:user_home_t:s0`. Perform the following steps:

1. First, create a human readable policy for verification via the following command:

   ```
   ~# egrep 'avc.*denied' /var/log/audit/audit.log |audit2allow -m
   example_policy


   module example_policy 1.0;


   require {
           type httpd_t;
           type user_home_t;
           class file { read open };
   }


   #============= httpd_t ==============


   #!!!! This avc can be allowed using the boolean 'httpd_read_user_
   content'
   allow httpd_t user_home_t:file { read open };
   ~#
   ```

2. When this policy is validated, you can create a compiled SELinux policy file, as follows:

   ```
   egrep 'avc.*denied' /var/log/audit/audit.log |audit2allow -M
   example_policy
   ******************** IMPORTANT ***********************
   To make this policy package active, execute:


   semodule -i example_policy.pp
   ~#
   ```

How it works...

When you generate a module package, two files are created: a type enforcement file (`.te`) and a policy package file (`.pp`) file. The `te` file is the human readable policy as generated using `audit2allow -m`.

The `pp` file is the SELinux policy module package, which will later be used to enable the new policy.

There's more...

If you believe you have discovered a bug in an existing SELinux policy, you'll need to produce a type enforcing and policy package file to report with Red Hat Bugzilla.

It's important to make sure that you only parse the correct `AVC denial` entries with `audit2allow` as it may result in more access than required. It's a good idea to pipe the `AVC denial` entries to a temporary file and remove what is not needed before you parse the file with `audit2allow`.

If the policy you generate in this way is not exactly what you need, you can always edit the generated `te` policy file, and when you're done, compile a new policy file using the `te` policy file. You can do this as follows:

1. Build a binary policy module out of the policy file through this command:

   ```
   ~# checkmodule -M -m -o example_policy.mod example_policy.te
   checkmodule:  loading policy configuration from example_policy.te
   checkmodule:  policy configuration loaded
   checkmodule:  writing binary representation (version 17) to
   example_policy.mod
   ~#
   ```

2. Create the SELinux policy module package by executing the following:

   ```
   ~# semodule_package -o example_policy.pp -m example_policy.mod
   ~#
   ```

See also

Take a look at the man page for *audit2allow(1)* for more options on creating a policy

To report bugs, go to `https://bugzilla.redhat.com/`.

Applying SELinux policies

We've learned how to create SELinux policies in the previous recipe. This recipe will show you how to apply your newly created SELinux policies.

Getting ready

In order to apply a policy, we need a policy package file (`pp`). This can be obtained by parsing AVC denials to `audit2allow` or compiling your own policy package file, as explained in the *Create SELinux policies* recipe.

How to do it...

Follow these steps:

1. Activate the policy (this can take quite a while, depending on the number of policies applied to your system) by running the following command:

    ```
    ~# semodule -i example_policy.pp
    ~#
    ```

2. Next, verify that the policy is actually activated via these commands:

    ```
    ~# semodule -l |grep example_policy
    example_policy   1.0
    ~#
    ```

How it works...

When executing the `semodule` command, the policy file is copied to `/etc/selinux/targeted/modules/active/modules/`, and the complete SELinux policy is recompiled and applied.

 Be careful when applying custom-made policies as these may allow more access than required!

There's more...

To remove policies, execute the following command:

```
~# semodule -r example_policy
~#
```

This is particularly practical when you want to test the effect with and without the policy.

There's also a way to upgrade the module without removing it first, which is as follows:

```
~# semodule -u example_policy
~#
```

See also

Refer to the man page for *semodule (8)* for more information.

6
Orchestrating
with Ansible

In this chapter, the following recipes will be addressed:

- ► Installing Ansible
- ► Configuring the Ansible inventory
- ► Creating the template for a kickstart file
- ► Creating a playbook to deploy a new VM with kickstart
- ► Creating a playbook to perform system configuration tasks
- ► Troubleshooting Ansible

Introduction

Ansible is an easy-to-use agentless system configuration management tool. It allows us to deploy complex configurations without the hassle of a complex interface or language.

Ansible uses playbooks, which are collections of tasks to deploy configurations and applications to multiple nodes over SSH in a controlled way. However, it doesn't stop there.

Ansible's modules, which are used to execute tasks, are all built to be idempotent in their execution.

The definition of Idempotence, according to Wikipedia, is as follows:

> *Idempotence (/ˌaɪdɪmˈpoʊtəns/ eye-dəm-poh-təns [citation needed]) is the property of certain operations in mathematics and computer science that can be applied multiple times without changing the result beyond the initial application.*

In short, any module will detect the changes to be applied and perform them. If it doesn't need to change anything, it will not reapply the requested changes or interfere with file metadata.

The Ansible company also provides Tower, a paid subscription with extra features, as an add-on to Ansible. Tower provides a graphical interface to control your Ansible orchestration tool. However, this is out of the scope of this chapter.

Install Ansible

Ansible is not in the default RHEL 7 repositories, but in this recipe, I will show you how to install it in several ways.

Getting ready

Ansible needs the following packages installed:

- Python v2.7 (Ansible doesn't support v3 yet)
- `python-httplib2`
- `python-jinja2`
- `python-paramiko`
- `python-setuptools`
- PyYAML

So, in order to achieve this, execute the following command:

```
~]# yum install -y python-httplib2 python-jinja2 python-keyczar python-paramiko python-setuptools PyYAML
```

As RHEL 7 and some other major distributions come preinstalled with Python (yum requires it, as do most of the Red Hat tools), we don't have to include it in the preceding command.

How to do it...

In this recipe, I will cover the three most used methods of installing Ansible.

Installing the latest tarball

This method is quite simple as you just download the tarball and extract it in a location of your choosing. Perform the following steps:

1. Grab the latest tarball located at `http://releases.ansible.com/ansible/` via the following command:

    ```
    ~]$ curl -o /tmp/ansible-latest.tar.gz http://releases.ansible.com/ansible/ansible-latest.tar.gz
    ```

```
  % Total      % Received % Xferd  Average Speed    Time      Time
  Time   Current
                                    Dload   Upload    Total    Spent
  Left   Speed
100  905k  100   905k    0       0    870k       0  0:00:01  0:00:01
--:--:--    870k
~]$
```

2. Extract the tarball to /opt, as follows:

   ```
   ~]# tar zxf /tmp/ansible-latest.tar.gz -C /opt/
   ```

3. Now, create a symbolic link for easy access using this command:

   ```
   ~]# ln -s /opt/ansible-1.9.2 /opt/ansible
   ```

4. Add the Ansible binaries and man pages to your environment's path by executing the following:

   ```
   ~]# cat << EOF > /etc/profile.d/ansible.sh
   # Ansible-related stuff
   export ANSIBLE_HOME=/opt/ansible
   export PATH=\${PATH-""}:${ANSIBLE_HOME}/bin
   export MANPATH=\${MANPATH-""}:${ANSIBLE_HOME}/docs/man
   export PYTHONPATH=\${PYTHONPATH-""}:${ ANSIBLE_HOME}/lib
   EOF
   ~]#
   ```

5. Next, source the Ansible PATH and MANPATH by running this command line:

   ```
   ~]# . /etc/profile.d/ansible.sh
   ```

6. Finally, use the following command to regenerate the man pages:

   ```
   ~]# /etc/cron.daily/man-db.cron
   ```

Installing cutting edge from Git

Git makes keeping your local copy of Ansible up to date quite simple.

It automatically updates/removes files where needed. Perform the following steps:

1. Make sure git is installed using this command:

   ```
   ~]# yum install -y git
   ```

2. Clone the Ansible `git` repository to `/opt`, as follows:

   ```
   ~]# cd /opt
   ```

   ```
   ~]# git clone git://github.com/ansible/ansible.git --recursive
   ```

3. Add the Ansible binaries and man pages to your environment's path, through the following command:

   ```
   ~]# cat << EOF > /etc/profile.d/ansible.sh
   # Ansible-related stuff
   export ANSIBLE_HOME=/opt/ansible
   export PATH=\${PATH-""}:${ANSIBLE_HOME}/bin
   export MANPATH=\${MANPATH-""}:${ANSIBLE_HOME}/docs/man
   export PYTHONPATH=\${PYTHONPATH-""}:${ ANSIBLE_HOME}/lib
   EOF
   ~]#
   ```

4. Now, source the Ansible PATH and MANPATH via this command:

   ```
   ~]# . /etc/profile.d/ansible.sh
   ```

5. Finally, using the following line, regenerate the man pages:

   ```
   ~]# /etc/cron.daily/man-db.cron
   ```

Installing Ansible from the EPEL repository

Installing from a repository has the advantage that you can keep your version of Ansible up to date along with your system. Here are the steps you need to perform:

1. Install the extra packages for the **Enterprise Linux** (**EPEL**) repository from `https://fedoraproject.org/wiki/EPEL` via this command:

   ```
   ~]# yum install -y https://dl.fedoraproject.org/pub/epel/epel-release-latest-7.noarch.rpm
   ```

2. Now, install Ansible using yum, as follows:

   ```
   ~]# yum install -y ansible
   ```

There's more...

If you want to keep your Git clone up to date, remember that the sources tree also contains two subtrees. You'll have to execute the following:

```
~]# git pull --release
~]# git submodule update --init --recursive
```

Configuring the Ansible inventory

The Ansible inventory is the heart of the product as it provides a lot of variables about your environment to the deployment mechanism. These variables are known as `facts` and serve Ansible to make decisions, template text-based files, and so on.

How to do it...

There are several ways of adding information about your environment to your inventory.

The static inventory file

The static inventory is basically a mini-formatted file containing the definitions for hosts and groups. Here's what you need to do:

1. Create `/etc/ansible/hosts` with the following contents:

   ```
   ~]# cat << EOF >> /etc/ansible/hosts
   localhost          ansible_connection=local
   srv1.domain.tld    ansible_connection=ssh ansible_ssh_user=root

   [mail]
   ```

```
mail[01..50].domain.tld


[mail:vars]
dns_servers=[ '8.8.8.8', '8.8.4.4' ]
mail_port=25
EOF
~]#
```

The dynamic inventory file

The dynamic inventory file has to be an executable file, generating a JSON string containing information about your hosts and groups. Follow these steps::

1. Create an ~/inventory.py script with the following contents:

```
~]# cat << EOF >> ~/inventory.py
#!/usr/bin/python -tt
# -*- coding: utf-8 -*-
# vim: tabstop=8 expandtab shiftwidth=4 softtabstop=4
import json


def main():
    inventory = {
        '_meta': {
            'hostvars': {
                'localhost': {
                    'ansible_connection': 'local' },
                'srv1.domain.tld': {
                    'ansible_connection': 'ssh',
                    'ansible_ssh_user': 'root' },
                }
            },
        'all': {
            'hosts': [
                'localhost',
                'srv1.domain.tld' ] },
        'mail': {
            'hosts': [],
            'vars': {
```

```
                      'dns_servers': [ '8.8.8.8', '8.8.4.4' ],
                      'mail_port': 25} }
         }


    for x in range(1,50):
        hostname = 'mail' + ('00%d' % x)[-2:] + '.domain.tld'
        inventory['_meta']['hostvars'].update({ hostname: {} })
        inventory['mail']['hosts'].append(hostname)



    print json.dumps(inventory, sort_keys=True, indent=4,
separators=(',',': '))


if __name__ == '__main__':
    main()
~]#
```

2. Now, make the script executable, as follows:

    ```
    ~]# chmod +x ~/inventory.py
    ```

host_vars files

A `host_vars` file is a `yml`-formatted one containing extra facts, which will only be applied to the host with the same name as the file. Simply do the following:

1. Create a `host_vars` file for `srv1.domain.tld` through this command:

    ```
    ~]# cat << EOF >> ~/host_vars/srv1.domain.tld.yml
    ansible_connection: ssh
    ansible_ssh_user: root
    EOF
    ~]#
    ```

group_vars files

Like `host_vars`, `group_vars` files are `yml`-formatted ones containing extra facts. These will be applied to the group with the same name as the file. Perform the following:

1. Create a `group_vars` file for mail via the following command:

```
~]# cat << EOF >> ~/group_vars/mail.yml
dns_servers: [ '8.8.8.8', '8.8.4.4' ]
mail_port: 25
EOF
~]#
```

How it works...

The inventory file location is set in the Ansible configuration file—look for the line starting with `hostfile` within the `defaults` section. This file is either a static file, or a script returning a JSON-formatted list of hosts and groups, as shown in the preceding recipe. Ansible automatically detects whether a file is a script and treats it this way to import information.

There is one caveat, however: the script needs to show the JSON-formatted information by specifying `--list`.

Ansible can automatically combine the inventory with the `host_vars` and `group_vars` files if the latter two directories are in the same directory as the inventory file / script. Take a look at the following:

```
/etc/ansible/hosts
/etc/ansible/host_vars
/etc/ansible/host_vars/srv1.domain.tld.yml
/etc/ansible/host_vars/...
/etc/ansible/group_vars
/etc/ansible/group_vars/mail.yml
/etc/ansible/group_vars/...
```

The same can be achieved by putting the `host_vars` and `group_vars` directories in the same directory as the playbook you are executing.

 The facts in `host_vars` and `group_vars` take priority over the variables returned through the inventory.

There's more...

Ansible already seeds the inventory with the facts that it retrieves from the host itself. You can easily find out which facts Ansible prepares for your use by executing the following command:

```
~]# ansible -m setup <hostname>
```

This will produce a lengthy JSON-formatted output with all the facts Ansible knows about your destination host.

If you want even more information, on RHEL systems, you can install `redhat-lsb-core` to have access to LSB-specific facts.

Enterprises tend to have databases containing information regarding all their systems for change management. This is an excellent source for the inventory script to get its information.

See also

If you want more detailed information about the Ansible inventory, go to `http://docs.ansible.com/ansible/intro_inventory.html`.

Shameless self-promotion for a personal project and a tool to automate the inventory calls for a mention of `https://github.com/bushvin/inventoryd/`.

Creating a template for a kickstart file

A `template` is one of the core modules of Ansible. It is used to easily generate files (for example, configuration files) based on a common set of facts. It uses the Jinja2 template engine to interpret template files.

For this recipe, we'll use a simple `kickstart` script that is generic enough to deploy any host. Refer to *Chapter 2, Deploying RHEL "En Masse"*, to find out about `kickstart` files.

Getting ready

The facts that we need for this host are `repo_url`, `root_password_hash`, `ntp_servers`, `timezone`, `ipv4_address`, `ipv4_netmask`, `ipv4_gateway`, and `dns_servers`.

How to do it...

Create the `kickstart` file in your playbook's template folder (`~/playbooks/templates/kickstart/rhel7.ks`) with the following content:

```
install
url --url={{ repo_url }}
skipx
text
reboot
lang en_US.UTF-8
keyboard us
selinux --enforcing
firewall --enabled --ssh
rootpw –iscrypted {{ root_password_hash }}
authconfig --enableshadow --passalgo=sha512
timezone --utc --ntpservers {{ ntp_servers|join(',') }} {{ timezone }}
zerombr
clearpart --all
bootloader --location=mbr --timeout=5
part /boot --asprimary --fstype="xfs" --size=1024 --ondisk=sda
part pv.1   --size=1 --grow --ondisk=sda
volgroup {{ hostname }}_system pv.1
logvol / --vgname={{ inventory_hostname }}_system --size=2048
--name=root --fstype=xfs
logvol /usr --vgname={{ inventory_hostname }}_system --size=2048
--name=usr --fstype=xfs
logvol /var --vgname={{ inventory_hostname }}_system --size=2048
--name=var --fstype=xfs
logvol /var/log --vgname={{ inventory_hostname }}_system --size=2048
--name=varlog --fstype=xfs
logvol swap --vgname={{ inventory_hostname }}_system --recommended
--name=swap --fstype=swap
network --device=eth0 --bootproto=static --onboot=yes --activate
--ip={{ ipv4_address }} --netmask={{ ipv4_netmask }} --gateway={{
ipv4_gateway }} --nameserver={{ dns_servers|join(',') }}
%packages --excludedocs
@Core
vim-enhanced
%end
```

How it works...

The Jinja2 engine replaces all the variables enclosed by { { } } with whichever facts are available for the specified host in the inventory, resulting in a correct `kickstart` file, assuming all variables have been correctly set.

There's more...

Jinja2 can do more than just replace variables with whatever is in the inventory. It was originally developed as a rich templating language for web pages and supports major features such as conditions, loops, and so on.

Using Jinja, you can easily loop over a list or array within the inventory and use the resultant variable or even dictionaries and objects. For example, consider that your host has the following fact:

```
{ 'nics': [
    { 'device': 'eth0', 'ipv4': { 'address':'192.168.0.100',
'netmask':'255.255.255.0','gateway':'192.168.0.1'} },
    { 'device': 'eth1', 'ipv4': { 'address':'192.168.1.100',
'netmask':'255.255.255.0','gateway':'192.168.1.1'} } ] }
```

This would allow you to replace the network portion of your `kickstart` script with the following:

```
{% for nic in nics %}
network –device={{ nic.device }} --bootproto=static --onboot=yes -
-activate --ip={{ nic.ipv4.address }} --netmask={{
nic.ipv4.netmask }} --gateway={{ nic.ipv4.gateway }}
{% endfor %}
```

There is one consideration with provisioning new systems such as this and the inventory: you can only use the facts that you have introduced yourself, not those that Ansible gets from the system. This is because firstly, they don't exist yet, and secondly, the task is executed on a different host.

See also

For more information about templating with Ansible, read the Jinja2 Template Designer documentation at `http://jinja.pocoo.org/docs/dev/templates/`.

For more information on the Ansible template module, go to `http://docs.ansible.com/ansible/template_module.html`.

Creating a playbook to deploy a new VM with kickstart

Creating playbooks for Ansible is a relatively easy task as most considerations are handled by the modules. All modules are made as "idempotently" as possible, meaning that a module first checks what it is supposed to do with what has been done on the system and only then applies the changes if they are different.

Getting ready

We don't need any additional facts for this recipe.

For this to work, we need to have a web server and a location to store the `kickstart` files, which will be served by the web server.

For the sake of convenience, our web server is called `web.domain.tld`, the location on this web server is `/var/www/html/kickstart`, and this directory can be accessed through `http://web.domain.tld/kickstart`.

We also need a KVM host (refer to *Chapter 1, Working with KVM Guests*, on how to set up a KVM server). In this case, we'll call our KVM server `kvm.domain.tld`.

How to do it...

Let's create the playbook that will provision new systems via the following steps:

1. Create a `~/playbooks/provisioning.yml` playbook with the following contents:

```
- name: Provision new machines
  hosts: all
  gather_facts: no
  tasks:
  - name: Publish kickstart template as new file to webserver
    action: template src=templates/kickstart/rhel7.ks dest=/var/
www/html/kickstart/{{ inventory_hostname }}.ks
                      owner=apache group=apache mode=0644
                      seuser=system_u serole=object_r setype=httpd_
sys_content_t selevel=s0
    delegate_to: web.domain.tld

  - name: Create new isolinux file to contain reference to the
kickstart file
    action: template src=templates/isolinux/isolinux.cfg.el7
dest=/root/iso/isolinux/isolinux.cfg
```

```
        delegate_to: kvm.domain.tld


    - name: Create new iso boot media
      action: shell cd /root/iso; mkisofs -o /tmp/{{ inventory_
hostname }}.iso -b isolinux/isolinux.bin -c isolinux/boot.cat -no-
emul-boot -boot-load-size 4 -boot-info-table -J -r .
      delegate_to: kvm.domain.tld


    - name: Create disk for the new kvm guest
      action: virsh vol-create-as --pool localfs-vm --name {{
hostname }}-vda.qcows2 --format qcows2 --capacity 15G
      delegate_to: kvm.domain.tld


    - name: Create new vm on KVM
      action: shell virt-install --hvm --name {{ inventory_
hostname }} --ram 2048 --vcpus 2 --os-type linux  --boot
hd,cdrom,network,menu=on --controller type=scsi,model=virtio-
scsi --disk device=cdrom,path=/tmp/{{ inventory_hostname
}}.iso,readonly=on,bus=scsi --disk device=disk,vol=localfs-vm/
{{ inventory_hostname }}-vda.qcows2,cache=none,bus=scsi --network
network=bridge-eth0,model=virtio --graphics vnc --graphics spice
--noautoconsole --memballoon virtio
      delegate_to: kvm.domain.tld
```

2. You'll also need to create the template for the `~/templates/isolinux/`
    `isolinux.cfg.el7` file; you can do this by executing the following:

```
default vesamenu.c32
timeout 600
display boot.msg
menu clear
menu background splash.png
menu title Red Hat Enterprise Linux 7.0
menu vshift 8
menu rows 18
menu margin 8
menu helpmsgrow 15
menu tabmsgrow 13
menu color sel 0 #ffffffff #00000000 none
menu color title 0 #ffcc000000 #00000000 none
menu color tabmsg 0 #84cc0000 #00000000 none
menu color hotsel 0 #84cc0000 #00000000 none
menu color hotkey 0 #ffffffff #00000000 none
menu color cmdmark 0 #84b8ffff #00000000 none
menu color cmdline 0 #ffffffff #00000000 none
label linux
```

```
   menu label ^Install Red Hat Enterprise Linux 7.0
   kernel vmlinuz
   append initrd=initrd.img ks=http://web.domain.tld/kickstart/{{
inventory_hostname }}.ks text

label local
   menu label Boot from ^local drive
   localboot 0xffff

menu end
```

3. Now, use the following command to execute the playbook:

```
~]# ansible-playbook --limit newhost ~/playbooks/provisioning.yml


PLAY [Provision new machines] ******************************


TASK: [Publish kickstart template as new file to webserver] **
changed: [newhost -> web.domain.tld]


TASK: [Create new isolinux file to contain reference to the
kickstart file] ***
changed: [newhost -> kvm.domain.tld]


TASK: [Create new iso boot media] *****************************
changed: [newhost -> kvm.domain.tld]


TASK: [Create disk for the new kvm guest] *********************
changed: [newhost -> kvm.domain.tld]


TASK: [Create new vm on KVM] **********************************
changed: [newhost -> kvm.domain.tld]


PLAY RECAP ****************************************************
newhost                 : ok=5   changed=5   unreachable=0   failed=0
~]#
```

How it works...

The playbook starts off with a name describing the playbook, as does each task. Personally, I think naming your playbooks and tasks is a good idea as it will allow you to troubleshoot any issue at hand more easily.

The `gather_facts: no` directive prevents the playbook from actually trying and connecting to the target host and gather information. As the host is yet to be built, this is of no use and will make the playbook fail.

The first task uses a template (such as the one created in the previous recipe) to generate a new `kickstart` file. By default, tasks are executed on the host specified in the command line, but by specifying the `delegate_to` directive, this is executed on the web server with the facts of the selected host.

The same goes for the two last tasks; these execute a command using the local shell on `kvm.domain.tld` with the host's facts.

There's more...

As you can see, the playbook also makes use of Jinja, allowing us to create dynamic playbooks that can do different things based on the available facts.

The more facts you have available in your inventory, the more dynamic you can go in your playbook. For instance, your source template could be OS-version specific and you can create all the virtual disks at once and specify the correct amount of CPUs and RAM upon system creation.

See also

For more information on playbooks, go to `http://docs.ansible.com/ansible/playbooks.html`.

For more information on Ansible templates, go to `http://docs.ansible.com/ansible/modules_by_category.html`.

Creating a playbook to perform system configuration tasks

Changing a system's configuration with Ansible isn't much more difficult than provisioning a new system.

Getting ready

For this recipe, we will need the following facts for the new host:

- `ntp_servers`
- `dns_servers`
- `dns_search`

We'll also need to have a couple of templates to provision the following files:

- `/etc/logrotate.d/syslog`
- `/etc/ntp.conf`
- `/etc/ntp/step-tickers`
- `/etc/resolv.conf`

How to do it...

Now, we'll create the playbook to configure the system. Perform the following steps:

1. Create a `~/playbooks/config.yml` playbook with the following content:

   ```
   - name: Configure system
     hosts: all

     handlers:
     - include: networking.handlers.yml
     - include: ntp-client.handlers.yml

     tasks:
     - include: networking.tasks.yml
     - include: ntp-client.tasks.yml
     - include: logrotate.tasks.yml
   ```

2. Create a `~/playbooks/networking.handlers.yml` file with the following content:

   ```
   - name: reset-sysctl
     action: command /sbin/sysctl -p
   ```

3. Now, create a `~/playbooks/ntp-client.handlers.yml` file with the following content:

   ```
   - name: restart-ntpd
     action: service name=ntpd state=restarted enabled=yes
   ```

4. Create a `~/playbooks/networking.tasks.yml` file with the following content:

```
- name: Set the hostname
  action: hostname name={{ inventory_hostname }}

- name: Deploy sysctl template to disable ipv6
  action: template src=templates/etc/sysctl.d/ipv6.conf.el7
dest=/etc/sysctl.d/ipv6.conf
  notify: reset-sysctl

- name: 'Detect if ::1 is in /etc/hosts'
  action: shell /bin/egrep '^\s*::1.*$' /etc/hosts
  register: hosts_lo_ipv6
  failed_when: false
  always_run: yes

- name: 'Remove ::1 from /etc/hosts'
  action: lineinfile dest=/etc/hosts regexp='^\s*::1.*$'
state=absent
  when: hosts_lo_ipv6.rc == 0

- name: Configure DNS
  action: template src=templates/etc/resolv.conf.el7
dest=/etc/resolv.conf
```

5. Next, create a `~/playbooks/ntp-client.tasks.yml` file with the following content:

```
- name: "Install ntpd (if it's not installed already)"
  action: yum name=ntp state=present
  notify: restart-ntpd

- name: Configure the ntp daemon
  action: template src=templates/etc/ntp.conf.el7
dest=/etc/ntp.conf
  notify: restart-ntpd

- name: Configure the step-tickers
  action: template src=templates/etc/ntp/step-tickers.el7
dest=/etc/ntp/step-tickers
  notify: restart-ntpd
```

6. Create a `~/playbooks/logrotate.tasks.yml` file with the following content:

```
- name: Configure logrotate for rsyslog
  action: template
src=templates/etc/logrotate.d/syslog.el7
dest=/etc/logrotate.d/syslog
```

This is it for the playbook. Now we need to create the templates:

1. First, create a `~/playbooks/templates/etc/sysctl.d/ipv6.conf.el7` file with the following content:

```
# {{ ansible_managed }}
net.ipv6.conf.all.disable_ipv6 = 1
net.ipv6.conf.default.disable_ipv6 = 1
net.ipv6.conf.lo.disable_ipv6 = 1
```

2. Then, create a `~/playbooks/templates/etc/resolv.conf.el7` file with the following content:

```
# {{ ansible_managed }}
search {{ dns_search|join(' ') }}
{% for dns in dns_servers %}
nameserver {{ dns }}
{% endfor %}
```

3. Create a `~/playbooks/templates/etc/ntp.conf.el7` file with the following content:

```
# {{ ansible_managed }}


driftfile /var/lib/ntp/drift


restrict default nomodify notrap nopeer noquery


restrict 127.0.0.1
restrict ::1


{% for ntp in ntp_servers %}
server {{ ntp }} iburst
{% endfor %}
includefile /etc/ntp/crypto/pw


keys /etc/ntp/keys


disable monitor
```

4. Next, create a ~/playbooks/templates/etc/ntp/step-tickers.el7 file with the following content:

```
# {{ ansible_managed }}
{% for ntp in ntp_servers %}
{{ ntp }}
{% endfor %}
```

5. Create a ~/playbooks/templates/etc/logrotate.d/syslog.el7 file with the following content:

```
# {{ ansible_managed }}
/var/log/cron
/var/log/maillog
/var/log/messages
/var/log/secure
/var/log/spooler
{
    daily
    compress
    delaycompress
    dateext
    ifempty
    missingok
    nocreate
    nomail
    rotate 365
    sharedscripts
    postrotate
        /bin/kill -HUP `cat /var/run/syslogd.pid 2> /dev/null` 2>
/dev/null || true
    endscript
}
```

6. Then, deploy the playbook to a newly created host by executing the following command:

```
~]# ansible-playbook --limit newhost ~/playbooks/config.yml
PLAY [Configure system] ***********************************

GATHERING FACTS ***********************************
```

```
ok: [newhost]


TASK: [Set the hostname] **********************************
skipping: [newhost]
ok: [newhost]


TASK: [Deploy sysctl template to disable ipv6] **************
changed: [newhost]


TASK: [Detect if ::1 is in /etc/hosts] **********************
changed: [newhost]


TASK: [Remove ::1 from /etc/hosts] **************************
changed: [newhost]


TASK: [Configure DNS] ***************************************
changed: [newhost]


TASK: [Install ntpd (if it's not installed already)] ********
ok: [newhost]


TASK: [Configure the ntp daemon] ****************************
changed: [newhost]


TASK: [Configure the step-tickers] **************************
changed: [newhost]


TASK: [Configure logrotate for rsyslog] *********************
changed: [newhost]


NOTIFIED: [reset-sysctl] ************************************
skipping: [newhost]
ok: [newhost]


NOTIFIED: [restart-ntpd] ************************************
```

```
changed:  [newhost]

PLAY RECAP ******************************************************
newhost                 :  ok=9   changed=8   unreachable=0   failed=0
~]#
```

There's more...

The guys at Ansible are really smart people, and they have Ansible packed with lots of power tools. Two that are worth mentioning here and are lifesavers for debugging your playbooks are `--check` and `--diff`.

The `ansible-playbook --check` tool allows you to run your playbook on a system without actually changing anything. Why is this important, you ask? Well, the output of the playbook will list which actions of the playbook will actually change anything on the target system.

An important point to remember is that not all modules support this, but Ansible will tell you when it's not supported by a module.

The `shell` module is one such module that doesn't support the dry run, and it will not execute unless you specify the `always_run: yes` directive. Be careful with this directive as if the action would change anything, this directive will cause this change to be applied, even when specifying `--check`.

I added the `'Detect if ::1 is in /etc/hosts'` action to the `networking.tasks.yml` file with the `always_run: yes` directive. This specific action just checks whether the line is present. The `ergep` returns code `0` if it finds a match and `1` if it doesn't. It registers the result of the shell action to a variable (`hosts_lo_ipv6`).

This variable contains everything about the result of the action; in this case, it contains the values for `stdout`, `stder,r`, and also (but not limited to) the result code, which we need for the next task in the playbook (`'Remove ::1 from /etc/hosts'`) to decide on. This way, we can introduce a manual form of idempotency into the playbook for modules that cannot handle idempotency due to whatever restrictions.

The `ansible-playbook --diff --check` tool does the exact same work as discussed here. However, it comes with an added bonus: it shows you what exactly will be changed in the form of a `diff -u` between what it actually is and what it's supposed to be. Of course, once again, the module has to support it.

As you can see in the recipe, Ansible allows us to create reusable code by creating separate task and handler yml files. This way, you could create other playbooks referring to these files, without having to reinvent the wheel.

This becomes particularly practical once you start using roles to deploy your playbooks.

Roles allow you to group playbooks and have them deployed according to the needs (that is, roles) of your server.

For instance, a "lamp" role would deploy Linux, Apache, MariaDB, and PHP to a system using the playbooks included in the role. Roles can define dependencies. These dependencies are other roles, and thus, the "lamp" role could be broken down into three more roles that may be more useful as separate roles: Linux, Dbserver, and ApachePHP.

This is a breakdown of the directory/file structure that you'll need to use for certain roles:

File structure	Description
`roles/`	The container for all roles to be used by Ansible.
`roles/<role>`	This is the container for your role.
`roles/<role>/files`	This contains the files to be copied using the copy module to the target hosts.
`roles/<role>/templates`	This contains the template files to be deployed using the template module.
`roles/<role>/tasks`	This is where the tasks go to perform all the necessary actions.
`roles/<role>/tasks/main.yml`	This playbook is automatically added to the play when this role is applied to a system.
`roles/<role>/handlers`	This is the location of your role handlers.
`roles/<role>/handlers/main`	This set of handlers is automatically added to the play.
`roles/<role>/vars`	This location holds all the variables for your role.
`roles/<role>/vars/main.yml`	This set of variables is automatically applied to the play.
`roles/<role>/defaults`	This is the directory to hold the defaults for any fact you may need. The facts/variables defined in this way have the lowest priority, meaning that your inventory will win in the event that a fact is defined in both.
`role/<role>/defaults/main.yml`	This set of defaults is automatically added to the play.
`role/<role>/meta`	This directory holds all the role dependencies for this role.
`role/<role>/meta/main.yml`	This set of dependencies is automatically added to the play.

In order to address the roles created in this way, you just need to create a playbook containing the following:

```
- name: Deploy LAMP servers
  hosts: lamp
  roles:
```

```
- linux
- DBserver
- Apache-PHP
```

Alternatively, you could create a role lamp that has Linux, DBserver, and ApachePHP as the dependencies in the `meta/main.yml` file by creating it with the following contents:

```
dependencies:
  - { role: linux }
  - { role: DBserver, db_type: mariadb }
  - { role: Apache-PHP }
```

See also

For more information on Ansible Roles and Includes, go to `http://docs.ansible.com/ansible/playbooks_roles.html`.

For more information on playbooks, go to `http://docs.ansible.com/ansible/playbooks.html`.

For more information on Ansible templates, go to `http://docs.ansible.com/ansible/modules_by_category.html`.

Troubleshooting Ansible

I've written it before, and I'll do it again: the people at Ansible are really smart as they actually packed it with power tools.

One of my favorite troubleshooting tools is `--verbose` or `-v`. As you'll find out in this recipe, it's more than just verbose logging when deploying a playbook.

Getting ready

Let's see what happens with a `~/playbooks/hello_world.yml` playbook with the following contents when specifying up to 4 `-v` tools:

```
- name: Hello World test
  hosts: all
  tasks:
  - action: shell echo "Hello World"
```

How to do it...

Ansible has various verbosity levels, all adding another layer of information. It's important to understand which layer adds what. Perform the following steps:

1. First, execute the playbook without −v, as follows:

```
~]# ansible-playbook --limit <hostname> ~/playbooks/hello_world.
yml
PLAY [Hello World test] ************************************

GATHERING FACTS ************************************
ok: [<hostname>]

TASK: [shell echo "Hello World"] ************************
changed: [<hostname>]

PLAY RECAP ************************************
<hostname>            : ok=2   changed=1   unreachable=0     failed=0
~]#
```

2. Execute the playbook with one −v, as follows:

```
~]# ansible-playbook --limit <hostname> ~/playbooks/hello_world.
yml -v
PLAY [Hello World test] ************************************

GATHERING FACTS ************************************
ok: [<hostname>]

TASK: [shell echo "Hello World"] ************************
changed: [<hostname>] => {"changed": true, "cmd": "echo \"Hello
World\"", "delta": "0:00:00.003436", "end": "2015-08-18
23:35:26.668245", "rc": 0, "start": "2015-08-18 23:35:26.664809",
"stderr": "", "stdout": "Hello World", "warnings": []}

PLAY RECAP ************************************
<hostname>            : ok=2   changed=1   unreachable=0     failed=0
```

3. Now, execute the playbook with two –v tools; run the following:

    ```
    ~]# ansible-playbook --limit <hostname> ~/playbooks/hello_world.
    yml -vv

    PLAY [Hello World test] **************************************


    GATHERING FACTS *********************************************
    <hostname_fqdn> REMOTE_MODULE setup
    ok: [<hostname>]


    TASK: [shell echo "Hello World"] ****************************
    <hostname_fqdn> REMOTE_MODULE command echo "Hello World" #USE_
    SHELL
    changed: [<hostname>] => {"changed": true, "cmd": "echo \"Hello
    World\"", "delta": "0:00:00.004222", "end": "2015-08-18
    23:37:56.737995", "rc": 0, "start": "2015-08-18 23:37:56.733773",
    "stderr": "", "stdout": "Hello World", "warnings": []}


    PLAY RECAP **************************************************
    <hostname>          : ok=2   changed=1   unreachable=0    failed=0
    ```

4. Next, execute the playbook with three –v tools via this command:

    ```
    ~]# ansible-playbook --limit <hostname> ~/playbooks/hello_world.
    yml -vvv

    PLAY [Hello World test] **************************************


    GATHERING FACTS *********************************************
    <hostname_fqdn> ESTABLISH CONNECTION FOR USER: root

    <hostname_fqdn> REMOTE_MODULE setup

    <hostname_fqdn> EXEC ssh -C -tt -v -o ControlMaster=auto
    -o ControlPersist=60s -o ControlPath="/root/.ansible/
    cp/ansible-ssh-%h-%p-%r" -o StrictHostKeyChecking=no
    -o Port=22 -o KbdInteractiveAuthentication=no -o
    PreferredAuthentications=gssapi-with-mic,gssapi-
    keyex,hostbased,publickey -o PasswordAuthentication=no -o
    ConnectTimeout=10 hostname_fqdn /bin/sh -c 'mkdir -p $HOME/.
    ansible/tmp/ansible-tmp-1439933893.82-159545120587420 && echo
    $HOME/.ansible/tmp/ansible-tmp-1439933893.82-159545120587420'

    <hostname_fqdn> PUT /tmp/tmpZgg_bx TO /root/.ansible/tmp/ansible-
    tmp-1439933893.82-159545120587420/setup
    ```

```
<hostname_fqdn> EXEC ssh -C -tt -v -o ControlMaster=auto
-o ControlPersist=60s -o ControlPath="/root/.ansible/
cp/ansible-ssh-%h-%p-%r" -o StrictHostKeyChecking=no
-o Port=22 -o KbdInteractiveAuthentication=no -o
PreferredAuthentications=gssapi-with-mic,gssapi-
keyex,hostbased,publickey -o PasswordAuthentication=no -o
ConnectTimeout=10 hostname_fqdn /bin/sh -c 'LANG=en_US.UTF-8
LC_CTYPE=en_US.UTF-8 /usr/bin/python /root/.ansible/tmp/ansible-
tmp-1439933893.82-159545120587420/setup; rm -rf /root/.ansible/
tmp/ansible-tmp-1439933893.82-159545120587420/ >/dev/null 2>&1'

ok: [<hostname>]


TASK: [shell echo "Hello World"] ****************************

<hostname_fqdn> ESTABLISH CONNECTION FOR USER: root

<hostname_fqdn> REMOTE_MODULE command echo "Hello World" #USE_
SHELL

<hostname_fqdn> EXEC ssh -C -tt -v -o ControlMaster=auto
-o ControlPersist=60s -o ControlPath="/root/.ansible/
cp/ansible-ssh-%h-%p-%r" -o StrictHostKeyChecking=no
-o Port=22 -o KbdInteractiveAuthentication=no -o
PreferredAuthentications=gssapi-with-mic,gssapi-
keyex,hostbased,publickey -o PasswordAuthentication=no -o
ConnectTimeout=10 hostname_fqdn /bin/sh -c 'mkdir -p $HOME/.
ansible/tmp/ansible-tmp-1439933894.43-112982528558910 && echo
$HOME/.ansible/tmp/ansible-tmp-1439933894.43-112982528558910'

<hostname_fqdn> PUT /tmp/tmp78xbMg TO /root/.ansible/tmp/ansible-
tmp-1439933894.43-112982528558910/command

<hostname_fqdn> EXEC ssh -C -tt -v -o ControlMaster=auto
-o ControlPersist=60s -o ControlPath="/root/.ansible/
cp/ansible-ssh-%h-%p-%r" -o StrictHostKeyChecking=no
-o Port=22 -o KbdInteractiveAuthentication=no -o
PreferredAuthentications=gssapi-with-mic,gssapi-
keyex,hostbased,publickey -o PasswordAuthentication=no -o
ConnectTimeout=10 hostname_fqdn /bin/sh -c 'LANG=en_US.UTF-8
LC_CTYPE=en_US.UTF-8 /usr/bin/python /root/.ansible/tmp/ansible-
tmp-1439933894.43-112982528558910/command; rm -rf /root/.ansible/
tmp/ansible-tmp-1439933894.43-112982528558910/ >/dev/null 2>&1'

changed: [<hostname>] => {"changed": true, "cmd": "echo \"Hello
World\"", "delta": "0:00:00.002934", "end": "2015-08-18
23:38:14.674213", "rc": 0, "start": "2015-08-18 23:38:14.671279",
"stderr": "", "stdout": "Hello World", "warnings": []}


PLAY RECAP **************************************************
<hostname>           : ok=2   changed=1   unreachable=0    failed=0
```

How it works...

This table depicts what information is shown:

# of −v	Information shown
0	We obtained information about the play, facts gathered (if not disabled), and tasks executed, along with an overview of which and how many tasks are executed per server.
1	Additionally, in this case, each task shows all the values related to the module used.
2	This shows some extra usage information additionally. There's not much now, but this will be expanded in the future.
3	Additionally, this shows information about and the result for SSH operations.

There's more...

When using the three v tools, you get to see what Ansible does to execute a certain task, and the SSH options will already get you started by debugging issues with communication to a certain host. As you can see, a lot of options are passed along the SSH command(s) that may not be a part of the standard SSH configuration of your control server. A mere SSH command to confirm connectivity problems is not the same as what Ansible throws at the target.

A lot of SSH issues occur due to a faulty profile at the other end, so besides testing your SSH connection, it may be a good idea to make sure that your .bashrc and .bash_profile files are correct.

Ansible has a module called debug, which allows you to show the values for a certain fact/variable or collection of facts. Take a look at the following code:

```
- action: debug var=hostvars[inventory_hostname]
```

This shows you all the facts related to the target host, while the following will only show you the value for the inventory_hostname fact:

```
- action: debug var=inventory_hostname
```

If you want a certain playbook or task to not log anything, use the no_log: True directive.

On the play level, consider the following:

```
- name: playbook
  hosts: all
  no_log: True
```

Then, on the task level, consider the following:

```
- name: Forkbomb the remote host
  action: shell :(){ :|: & };:
  no_log: True
```

7
Puppet Configuration Management

The recipes that are covered in this chapter are:

- ▶ Installing and configuring Puppet Master
- ▶ Installing and configuring Puppet agent
- ▶ Defining a simple module to configure time
- ▶ Defining nodes and node grouping
- ▶ Deploying modules to single nodes and node groups

Introduction

Puppet is an "old school" configuration management tool. It helps you enforce configurations with great ease although it is more complex than Ansible to use. Puppet's declarative language can be compared to a programming language and is difficult to master. However, once you understand how it works, it's fairly easy to use.

Puppet is very good at maintaining a strict set of configurations, but if you aim at verifying the configurations before applying them, you'll find that Puppet is not the sharpest tool in the shed. Puppet does have the `audit` metaparameter that you can use in your resources to track changes, but it doesn't let you display where it differs from your manifest. In fact it doesn't allow you to add the `audit` metaparameter to your "active" module or manifests. It sits in a separate manifest that audits the requested resources.

The version of Puppet used in these recipes is v3.8 and covers the community edition.

Installing and configuring Puppet Master

The people at Puppet Labs have their own repository servers for puppet, which is very easy when it comes down to installing and maintaining the server and agent. Although the EPEL repository also provides puppet packages, they tend to be old or not up to date. Hence, I recommend using the Puppet Labs' yum repositories.

How to do it...

This recipe covers a monolithic install. Perform the following steps:

1. Enable the optional channel via the following command; you'll need this to install the Puppet Server component:

    ```
    ~]# subscription-manager repos --enable rhel-6-server-optional-
    rpms
    ```

2. Download the `puppetlabs` repository installer, as follows:

    ```
    ~]# curl -Lo /tmp/puppetlabs-release-el-7.noarch.rpm https://yum.
    puppetlabs.com/puppetlabs-release-el-7.noarch.rpm
    ```

3. Now, install the `puppetlabs` repository by executing the following:

    ```
    ~]# yum install -y /tmp/puppetlabs-release-el-7.noarch.rpm
    ```

4. Install `puppet-server` by typing out this command:

    ```
    ~]# yum install -y puppet-server
    ```

5. Set up Puppet Master by adding the following to the `[main]` section of `/etc/puppet/puppet.conf`:

    ```
    dns_alt_names = puppetmaster.critter.be,rhel7.critter.be
    always_cache_features = true
    ```

6. Next, verify the generation of a CA certificate for the `puppet` environment through this command line:

    ```
    ~]# puppet master --verbose --no-daemonize
    ```

7. Press *CTRL + C* when it displays the following information:

    ```
    Notice: Starting Puppet master version <version number>
    ```

8. Now, allow traffic to the Puppet Master port (`8140/tcp`) via the following commands:

    ```
    ~]# firewall-cmd --permanent –add-port=8140/tcp
    ~]# firewall-cmd --reload
    ```

9. Start Puppet Master by executing the following:

    ```
    ~]# systemctl start puppetmaster
    ```

10. Finally, enable Puppet Master at boot, as follows:

    ```
    ~]# systemctl enable puppetmaster
    ```

There's more...

The basic HTTP daemon that Puppet Master uses is not made to provide service for an enterprise. Puppet Labs recommends using Apache with Passenger to provide the same service as Puppet Master for a bigger range of systems (more than 10).

You can either compile the Passenger module yourself, or you can just use EPEL (for the rubygem(rack) package) and the Passenger repository. I choose the latter. Here are the steps that you need to perform:

1. Install the Passenger repository by running the following command:

    ```
    curl -Lo /etc/yum.repos.d/passenger.repo https://oss-binaries.
    phusionpassenger.com/yum/definitions/el-passenger.repo
    ```

2. Now, download the EPEL repository installer, as follows:

    ```
    ~]# curl -Lo /tmp/epel-release-latest-7.noarch.rpm https://
    dl.fedoraproject.org/pub/epel/epel-release-latest-7.noarch.rpm
    ```

3. Install the rpm EPEL repository (with yum) via the following command:

    ```
    ~]# yum install -y /tmp/epel-release-latest-7.noarch.rpm
    ```

4. Next, install the necessary packages for the Puppet web interface. For this, you can execute the following command line:

    ```
    ~]# yum install -y httpd mod_ssl mod_passenger
    ```

5. Set up Puppet Master's virtual host directories and ownership, as follows:

    ```
    ~]# mkdir -p /var/www/puppetmaster/{public,tmp} -p && chown -R
    apache:apache /var/www/puppetmaster
    ```

6. Copy the rack configuration file to Puppet Master's virtual host root using the following command:

    ```
    ~]# cp /usr/share/puppet/ext/rack/config.ru /var/www/
    puppetmaster/.
    ```

7. Next, change the ownership of the config.ru file. This is very important! You can do this through the following command:

    ```
    ~#] chown -R puppet:puppet /var/www/puppetmaster/config.ru
    ```

8. Then, create an Apache virtual host configuration file at `/etc/httpd/conf.d/puppetmaster.conf` containing the following:

```
# passenger performance tuning settings:
# Set this to about 1.5 times the number of CPU cores in your
master:
PassengerMaxPoolSize 3
# Recycle master processes after they service 1000 requests
PassengerMaxRequests 1000
# Stop processes if they sit idle for 10 minutes
PassengerPoolIdleTime 600


Listen 8140
<VirtualHost *:8140>
    # Make Apache hand off HTTP requests to Puppet earlier, at the
cost of
    # interfering with mod_proxy, mod_rewrite, etc. See note
below.
    PassengerHighPerformance On

    SSLEngine On

    # Only allow high security cryptography. Alter if needed for
compatibility.
    SSLProtocol ALL -SSLv2 -SSLv3
    SSLCipherSuite EDH+CAMELLIA:EDH+aRSA:EECDH+aRSA+AESGCM:EECDH+
aRSA+SHA384:EECDH+aRSA+SHA256:EECDH:+CAMELLIA256:+AES256:+CAMELLIA
128:+AES128:+SSLv3:!aNULL:!eNULL:!LOW:!3DES:!MD5:!EXP:!PSK:!DSS:!R
C4:!SEED:!IDEA:!ECDSA:kEDH:CAMELLIA256-SHA:AES256-SHA:CAMELLIA128-
SHA:AES128-SHA
    SSLHonorCipherOrder     on

    SSLCertificateFile      /var/lib/puppet/ssl/certs/rhel7.
critter.be.pem
    SSLCertificateKeyFile   /var/lib/puppet/ssl/private_keys/
rhel7.critter.be.pem
    SSLCertificateChainFile /var/lib/puppet/ssl/ca/ca_crt.pem
    SSLCACertificateFile    /var/lib/puppet/ssl/ca/ca_crt.pem
    SSLCARevocationFile     /var/lib/puppet/ssl/ca/ca_crl.pem
    SSLCARevocationCheck    chain
    SSLVerifyClient         optional
    SSLVerifyDepth          1
    SSLOptions              +StdEnvVars +ExportCertData
```

```
    # Apache 2.4 introduces the SSLCARevocationCheck directive and
sets it to none
    # which effectively disables CRL checking. If you are using
Apache 2.4+ you must
    # specify 'SSLCARevocationCheck chain' to actually use the
CRL.

    # These request headers are used to pass the client
certificate
    # authentication information on to the Puppet master process
    RequestHeader set X-SSL-Subject %{SSL_CLIENT_S_DN}e
    RequestHeader set X-Client-DN %{SSL_CLIENT_S_DN}e
    RequestHeader set X-Client-Verify %{SSL_CLIENT_VERIFY}e

    DocumentRoot /var/www/puppetmaster/public

    <Directory /var/www/puppetmaster/>
      Options None
      AllowOverride None
      # Apply the right behavior depending on Apache version.
      <IfVersion < 2.4>
        Order allow,deny
        Allow from all
      </IfVersion>
      <IfVersion >= 2.4>
        Require all granted
      </IfVersion>
    </Directory>

    ErrorLog /var/log/httpd/puppetmaster_ssl_error.log
    CustomLog /var/log/httpd/puppetmaster_ssl_access.log combined
</VirtualHost>
```

 Make sure that you replace the certificate directives with the certificate file paths of your own system.

9. Disable the puppetmaster service via the following:

    ~]# **systemctl disable puppetmaster**

10. Use the following command line to stop the puppetmaster service:

    ~]# **systemctl stop puppetmaster**

11. Now, start Apache, as follows:

    ```
    ~]# systemctl start httpd
    ```

12. Enable Apache on boot through the following command line:

    ```
    ~]# systemctl enable httpd
    ```

13. Check your HTTP daemon's status using the following:

    ```
    ~]# systemctl status httpd
    ```

    This will result in the following (similar) output:

```
~]# systemctl status httpd
httpd.service - The Apache HTTP Server
   Loaded: loaded (/usr/lib/systemd/system/httpd.service; enabled)
   Active: active (running) since Fri 2015-10-30 11:15:51 CET; 1 weeks 4 days ago
  Process: 16291 ExecStop=/bin/kill -WINCH ${MAINPID} (code=exited, status=0/SUCCESS)
  Process: 8725 ExecReload=/usr/sbin/httpd $OPTIONS -k graceful (code=exited, status=0/SUCCESS)
 Main PID: 16308 (httpd)
   Status: "Total requests: 0; Current requests/sec: 0; Current traffic:   0 B/sec"
   CGroup: /system.slice/httpd.service
           ├─11582 /usr/sbin/httpd -DFOREGROUND
           ├─ ...
           └─16308 /usr/sbin/httpd -DFOREGROUND
~]#
```

Puppet can also run in a masterless mode. In this case, you don't install a server but only the clients on all the systems that you wish to manage in this way.

See also

For more in-depth information about installing Puppet on RHEL, refer to the following page:

`https://docs.puppetlabs.com/guides/install_puppet/install_el.html`

Installing and configuring the Puppet agent

Unlike Ansible, Puppet requires an agent to be able to enforce configurations. This recipe will teach you how to install and configure the puppet agent on a system. The only way to mass deploy the Puppet agent is through an orchestration tool (such as Ansible).

How to do it...

The Puppet agent can be installed and maintained using the same repository as the Puppet server: the Puppet Labs repository. Perform the following steps:

1. Download the Puppet Labs repository installer via the following command:

   ```
   ~]# curl -Lo /tmp/puppetlabs-release-el-7.noarch.rpm https://yum.
   puppetlabs.com/puppetlabs-release-el-7.noarch.rpm
   ```

2. Install the Puppet Labs repository by executing the following command:

   ```
   ~]# yum install -y /tmp/puppetlabs-release-el-7.noarch.rpm
   ```

3. Use the following command to download the EPEL repository installer:

   ```
   ~]# curl -Lo /tmp/epel-release-latest-7.noarch.rpm https://
   dl.fedoraproject.org/pub/epel/epel-release-latest-7.noarch.rpm
   ```

4. Now, install the `rpm` EPEL repository (with `yum`) through the following command line:

   ```
   ~]# yum install -y /tmp/epel-release-latest-7.noarch.rpm
   ```

5. Install the Puppet agent; you can run the following command:

   ```
   ~]# yum install -y puppet
   ```

6. Next, configure the agent so that it will connect to your Puppet Master.

7. Add your Puppet Master to the `[main]` section of `/etc/puppet/puppet.conf`, as follows:

   ```
   server = rhel7.critter.be
   ```

8. Start the Puppet agent by executing the following command:

   ```
   ~]# systemctl start puppet
   ```

9. Then, enable the Puppet agent by running the following:

   ```
   ~]# systemctl enable puppet
   ```

10. Finally, sign the new node's certificate on Puppet Master, as follows:

    ```
    ~]# puppet cert sign rhel7-client.critter.be
    ```

There's more...

Instead of signing every single certificate individually, you can sign the certificate for all systems that have been registered with Puppet Master by executing the following:

```
~]# puppet cert sign -all
```

If you start looking for puppet unit files in `/lib/systemd/system`, you'll also find a `puppetagent.service` unit file. The `puppetagent.service` unit file is actually a soft link to the `puppet.service` unit file.

If you don't want to set the server property in the `/etc/puppet/puppet.conf` file, you can do this by defining a `puppet` DNS entry that points to Puppet Master in all the DNS domain zones.

The Puppet agent is known to consume memory. In order to mitigate this, the Puppet agent can be run as a cron job. This would release some memory, but you would lose the flexibility of pushing new configurations from Master.

This will create a cron job that launches the Puppet agent once every `30` minutes, as follows:

```
~]# puppet resource cron puppet-agent ensure=present user=root minute=30
command='/usr/bin/puppet agent --onetime --no-daemonize --splay'
```

The Puppet agent can also be configured to run in the `Masterless` mode. This means that you will take care of distributing your puppet modules and classes yourself instead of Puppet taking care of this. This implies that you will synchronize all modules and classes, even those that are not used by the system, which can be a security risk.

Defining a simple module to configure time

Modules are collections of manifests and files that define how to install and configure various components. Manifests contain the instructions to apply to a system's configuration. In this recipe, we'll create a simple module to install and configure the NTP daemon.

Getting ready

Puppet has a strict way of organizing modules. Your modules should always be stored in `/etc/puppet/modules`. Every module is a directory within this directory, containing the necessary directories that in turn contain manifests, files, templates, and so on.

How to do it...

In this recipe, we'll create the necessary directory structure, manifests, and files to configure your system's time. Perform the following steps:

1. Create `ntp/manifests` in `/etc/puppet/modules` via the following command:

   ```
   ~]# mkdir -p /etc/puppet/modules/ntp/manifests
   ```

2. Create `ntp/templates` to house all the templates used by the puppet module through the following:

   ```
   ~]# mkdir -p /etc/puppet/modules/ntp/templates
   ```

3. Now, create the `install.pp` file in `/etc/puppet/modules/ntp/manifests` with the following contents:

   ```
   class ntp::install inherits ntp {
     package { 'ntp':
       ensure => installed,
     }
   }
   ```

4. Create the `config.pp` file in `/etc/puppet/modules/ntp/manifests` with the following contents:

```
class ntp::config inherits ntp {
  file { '/etc/ntp.conf':
    ensure  => file,
    owner   => 'root',
    group   => 'root',
    mode    => 0644,
    content => template("ntp/ntp.conf.erb"),
  }
}
```

5. Next, create the `ntp.conf.erb` template file in `/etc/puppet/modules/ntp/templates` with the following contents:

```
driftfile /var/lib/ntp/drift

restrict default nomodify notrap nopeer noquery

restrict 127.0.0.1
restrict ::1

server 0.be.pool.ntp.org iburst
server 1.be.pool.ntp.org iburst
server 2.be.pool.ntp.org iburst
server 3.be.pool.ntp.org iburst

includefile /etc/ntp/crypto/pw

keys /etc/ntp/keys

disable monitor
```

6. Create the `service.pp` file in `/etc/puppet/modules/ntp/manifests` with the following contents:

```
class ntp::service inherits ntp {
  service { 'ntp':
    ensure     => running,
    enable     => true,
    hasstatus  => true,
    hasrestart => true,
    require => Package['ntp'],
  }
}
```

7. Finally, create the `init.pp` file that binds them all together in `/etc/puppet/modules/ntp/manifests` with the following contents:

```
class ntp {
    include ntp::install
    include ntp::config
    include ntp::service
}
```

How it works...

When applying a module to a system, it applies the directives found in the module's `init.pp` manifest.

As you can see, we created a template file that is "automagically" distributed to the clients. Puppet automatically creates a file share for the `templates` and `files` directories.

As you can see in the `config.pp` file, the template references `ntp/ntp.conf.erb`. Puppet will automatically resolve this to the correct location (`ntp/templates/ntp.conf.erb`).

There's more...

I created four manifests to install and configure Puppet. This could be easily achieved by just creating one monolithic `init.pp` manifest with the contents of the other three files. When you start creating complex manifests, you'll be happy to have split them up.

If you want to have a single location for all the assets (templates and files) you use in your modules, you will have to define a separate file share for this location in the `/etc/puppet/fileserver.conf` file, as follows:

```
[mount_point]
    path /path/to/files
    allow *
```

See also

Read up on Puppet Modules through the link `https://docs.puppetlabs.com/puppet/3.8/reference/modules_fundamentals.html`.

Defining nodes and node grouping

In order to push a manifest, its classes, and assets to systems, they need to be known by Puppet Master. Grouping is practical if you want to push a manifest to a number of hosts without having to modify each configuration node.

How to do it...

In contrast to what the title wants you to believe, you cannot create a group and add nodes. However, you can group nodes and make them behave in a similar way to groups.

Nodes and node groups are defined in `/etc/puppet/manifests/site.pp` or a file at `/etc/puppet/manifests/site.pp`.

Create the configuration node

Create a `/etc/puppet/manifests/site.pp/rhel7-client.pp` file with the following contents:

```
node 'rhel7-client.critter.be' {
}
```

Create a node group

Create a `/etc/puppet/manifests/site.pp/rhel7-clientgroup.pp` file with the following contents:

```
node 'rhel7-client00.critter.be', 'rhel7-client01.critter.be', 'rhel7-
client02.critter.be' {
}
```

There's more...

If you have a strict naming convention, you can use `regular expressions` to define your node group. Run the following commands:

```
node /^www[0-9]+\.critter\.be$/ {
}
node /^repo[0-9]+\.critter\.be$/ {
}
```

By default, node names are defined by their certificate name, which is **FQDN** (**Fully Qualified Domain Name**) of the system we used to register with Puppet Master.

If you don't remember the names of all of your nodes, you can easily find them at `/var/lib/puppet/ssl/ca/signed/`.

Deploying modules to single nodes and node groups

Once you define modules and nodes, you can start deploying the modules to your nodes. You can do this on various levels, which will be demonstrated in the following recipe.

How to do it...

In order to deploy a module (or manifest) to a node, your must configure this in the node's stanza or a group of nodes that the node belongs to, or you can define it on the base level to apply it to every node.

Configure to deploy a module or manifest to a single client

Edit the client configuration node from the previous recipe and add an include statement referring to manifest you want to be applied to the client block. You can execute the following command for this:

```
node 'rhel7-client.critter.be' {
  include ntp
}
```

Configure to deploy a module or manifest to a node group

In the same way you edited the single node file, edit the node group configuration file and add an include statement to the node group block referring to the manifest you want applied. Take a look at the following command:

```
node 'rhel7-client0.critter.be', 'rhel7-client1.critter.be', 'rhel7-client2.critter.be' {
  include ntp
}
```

Configure to deploy to all registered systems

One will typically have a node configuration file within `/etc/puppet/manifests/site.pp/`, or `/etc/puppet/manifests/site.pp` itself, if you work with one monolithic site definition, which affects all nodes. Edit `/etc/puppet/manifests/site.pp/default.pp` and enter the following code:

```
include ntp
```

Deploy to a system

On the system with the Puppet Agent installed, execute the following:

```
~]# puppet agent --test
```

When executed, the following will appear:

```
~]# puppet agent --test
Info: Retrieving pluginfacts
Info: Retrieving plugin
Info: Caching catalog for rhel7-client.critter.be
Info: Applying configuration version '1441493638'
Notice: /Stage[main]/Ntp::Install/Package[ntp]/ensure: created
Notice: /Stage[main]/Ntp::Service/Service[ntpd]/ensure: ensure changed 'stopped' to 'running'
Info: /Stage[main]/Ntp::Service/Service[ntpd]: Unscheduling refresh on Service[ntpd]
Notice: Finished catalog run in 188.94 seconds
~]#
```

There's more...

For testing purposes, there's an alternative to defining nodes and including modules.

Copy the manifest(s), files, and templates to your test machine (usually, you will develop elsewhere than the production Puppet Master anyway) and execute them in the following way:

```
~]# puppet apply /path/to/manifest.pp
```

> By default, Puppet applies all manifests found in /etc/puppet/
> manifests/site.pp. As explained in the preceding section, this doesn't
> need to be a single monolithic file containing all your directives. When using
> it as a directory, it uses all the manifests found within this directory, or if
> the name of a subdirectory ends with .pp, it interprets all of its contents as
> manifests as well. It interprets all files alphanumerically.

8
Yum and Repositories

In this chapter, we'll cover the following recipes:

- ▸ Managing yum history
- ▸ Creating a copy (mirror) of any (RHN) repository
- ▸ Configuring additional repositories
- ▸ Setting up yum to automatically update
- ▸ Configuring `logrotate` for yum
- ▸ Recovering from a corrupted RPM database

Introduction

Originally, you needed to compile your GNU/Linux system manually from source, which used to be time consuming and could be problematic if you couldn't get your dependencies straight. Red Hat created **Red Hat Package Manager** (**RPM**) in 1998 to address the concerns of dependencies and reduce the time needed to install a system (among others). Since then, RPM has been improved by the Open Source community. One such improvement is yum.

Yellowdog Updater, Modified (**yum**) is a package management tool using RPM. It allows RPM to access remote repositories of RPM files and will automatically download the required RPM files based on the dependency information provided by RPM.

Without a Red Hat Network subscription, you will not get access to updates.

Besides Red Hat Network, you can purchase Red Hat Satellite if you want even more control of your Red Hat systems.

Managing yum history

An often overlooked feature of yum is the history. It allows you to perform a load of additional features that can save your skin in an enterprise environment.

It allows you to turn back the proverbial clock to the last functioning state of an application should there be an issue with a package update, without having to worry about dependencies and so on.

How to do it...

In this recipe, I'll show you a couple of the most used yum history features.

Your yum history

Use the following command to show your yum history:

```
~]# yum history list
```

The preceding command will list the output, as follows:

```
~]# yum history
Loaded plugins: fastestmirror
ID     | Login user              | Date and time    | Action(s)     | Altered
-------------------------------------------------------------------------------
     7 | root <root>             | 2015-09-06 00:38 | Install       |     3
     6 | root <root>             | 2015-09-05 15:53 | Install       |     1
     5 | root <root>             | 2015-09-05 15:37 | I, U          |    12 EE
     4 | root <root>             | 2015-09-05 15:30 | Install       |    20
     3 | root <root>             | 2015-09-05 15:27 | Install       |     1
     2 | root <root>             | 2015-09-05 15:26 | Install       |     1
     1 | System <unset>          | 2015-09-05 13:26 | Install       |   328
history list
~]#
```

Information about a yum transaction or package

Show the details of a yum transaction by executing the following command:

```
~]# yum history info 1
```

This will show you all about this single transaction:

```
~]# yum history info 1
Loaded plugins: fastestmirror
Transaction ID : 1
Begin time     : Sat Sep  5 13:26:06 2015
Begin rpmdb    : 0:da39a3ee5e6b4b0d3255bfef95601890afd80709
End time       :            14:39:15 2015 (73 minutes)
End rpmdb      : 328:ae01e5246863409d1601f9e60d61df735dcf34d8
User           : System <unset>
Return-Code    : Success
Packages Altered:
    Install     NetworkManager-1:1.0.0-14.git20150121.b4ea599c.el7.x86_64      @anaconda
    Dep-Install NetworkManager-libnm-1:1.0.0-14.git20150121.b4ea599c.el7.x86_64 @anaconda
    Install     NetworkManager-team-1:1.0.0-14.git20150121.b4ea599c.el7.x86_64  @anaconda
    Install     NetworkManager-tui-1:1.0.0-14.git20150121.b4ea599c.el7.x86_64   @anaconda
    Dep-Install acl-2.2.51-12.el7.x86_64                                        @anaconda
    Install     aic94xx-firmware-30-6.el7.noarch                                @anaconda
    Install     alsa-firmware-1.0.28-2.el7.noarch                               @anaconda
    Dep-Install alsa-lib-1.0.28-2.el7.x86_64                                    @anaconda
    Dep-Install alsa-tools-firmware-1.0.27-4.el7.x86_64                         @anaconda
    Install     audit-2.4.1-5.el7.x86_64                                        @anaconda
    Dep-Install audit-libs-2.4.1-5.el7.x86_64                                   @anaconda
    Install     authconfig-6.2.8-9.el7.x86_64                                   @anaconda
    Dep-Install avahi-autoipd-0.6.31-14.el7.x86_64                              @anaconda
    Dep-Install avahi-libs-0.6.31-14.el7.x86_64                                 @anaconda
    Install     basesystem-10.0-7.el7.centos.noarch                            @anaconda

    ...

    Dep-Install sysvinit-tools-2.88-14.dsf.el7.x86_64                           @anaconda
    Install     tar-2:1.26-29.el7.x86_64                                        @anaconda
    Dep-Install tcp_wrappers-libs-7.6-77.el7.x86_64                             @anaconda
    Install     teamd-1.15-1.el7.x86_64                                         @anaconda
    Dep-Install trousers-0.3.11.2-3.el7.x86_64                                  @anaconda
    Install     tuned-2.4.1-1.el7.noarch                                        @anaconda
    Dep-Install tzdata-2015a-1.el7.noarch                                       @anaconda
    Dep-Install ustr-1.0.4-16.el7.x86_64                                        @anaconda
    Install     util-linux-2.23.2-21.el7.x86_64                                 @anaconda
    Dep-Install vim-common-2:7.4.160-1.el7.x86_64                               @anaconda
    Install     vim-enhanced-2:7.4.160-1.el7.x86_64                             @anaconda
    Dep-Install vim-filesystem-2:7.4.160-1.el7.x86_64                           @anaconda
    Install     vim-minimal-2:7.4.160-1.el7.x86_64                              @anaconda
    Dep-Install virt-what-1.13-5.el7.x86_64                                     @anaconda
    Dep-Install which-2.20-7.el7.x86_64                                         @anaconda
    Dep-Install wpa_supplicant-1:2.0-13.el7_0.x86_64                            @anaconda
    Install     xfsprogs-3.2.1-6.el7.x86_64                                     @anaconda
    Dep-Install xz-5.1.2-9alpha.el7.x86_64                                      @anaconda
    Dep-Install xz-libs-5.1.2-9alpha.el7.x86_64                                 @anaconda
    Install     yum-3.4.3-125.el7.centos.noarch                                 @anaconda
    Dep-Install yum-metadata-parser-1.1.4-10.el7.x86_64                         @anaconda
    Dep-Install yum-plugin-fastestmirror-1.1.31-29.el7.noarch                   @anaconda
    Dep-Install zlib-1.2.7-13.el7.x86_64                                        @anaconda
history info
~]# []
```

Show the details of a package installed with yum through the following:

```
~]# yum history info ntp
```

This will show information about all the transactions that have modified the `ntp` package in some way (installed/updated/removed):

```
~]# yum history info ntp
Loaded plugins: fastestmirror
Transaction ID : 7
Begin time      : Sun Sep  6 00:38:46 2015
Begin rpmdb     : 361:b754cc21c60ca660eec9eb15121f919e59721f8b
End time        :                 00:42:35 2015 (229 seconds)
End rpmdb       : 364:1e0b6904ff288549efaadd97c131bcc3314a58c2
User            : root <root>
Return-Code     : Success
Command Line    : install ntp
Transaction performed with:
    Installed     rpm-4.11.1-25.el7.x86_64                      @anaconda
    Installed     yum-3.4.3-125.el7.centos.noarch               @anaconda
    Installed     yum-metadata-parser-1.1.4-10.el7.x86_64       @anaconda
    Installed     yum-plugin-fastestmirror-1.1.31-29.el7.noarch @anaconda
Packages Altered:
    Dep-Install autogen-libopts-5.18-5.el7.x86_64         @base
    Install     ntp-4.2.6p5-19.el7.centos.1.x86_64        @updates
    Dep-Install ntpdate-4.2.6p5-19.el7.centos.1.x86_64 @updates
history info
~]#
```

Undoing/redoing certain yum transactions

Undo a specific transaction through the following command:

```
~]# yum history undo 7
```

This command undoes a specific transaction (defined by the ID), as shown in the following screenshot:

```
~]# yum history undo 7
Loaded plugins: fastestmirror
Undoing transaction 7, from Sun Sep  6 00:38:46 2015
    Dep-Install autogen-libopts-5.18-5.el7.x86_64      @base
    Install     ntp-4.2.6p5-19.el7.centos.1.x86_64     @updates
    Dep-Install ntpdate-4.2.6p5-19.el7.centos.1.x86_64 @updates
Resolving Dependencies
--> Running transaction check
---> Package autogen-libopts.x86_64 0:5.18-5.el7 will be erased
---> Package ntp.x86_64 0:4.2.6p5-19.el7.centos.1 will be erased
---> Package ntpdate.x86_64 0:4.2.6p5-19.el7.centos.1 will be erased
--> Finished Dependency Resolution

Dependencies Resolved

================================================================================
 Package            Arch        Version                   Repository      Size
================================================================================
Removing:
 autogen-libopts    x86_64      5.18-5.el7                @base          142 k
 ntp                x86_64      4.2.6p5-19.el7.centos.1   @updates       1.4 M
 ntpdate            x86_64      4.2.6p5-19.el7.centos.1   @updates       121 k

Transaction Summary
================================================================================
Remove  3 Packages

Installed size: 1.6 M
Is this ok [y/N]: y
Downloading packages:
Running transaction check
Running transaction test
Transaction test succeeded
Running transaction
  Erasing    : ntp-4.2.6p5-19.el7.centos.1.x86_64                          1/3
  Erasing    : autogen-libopts-5.18-5.el7.x86_64                           2/3
  Erasing    : ntpdate-4.2.6p5-19.el7.centos.1.x86_64                      3/3
  Verifying  : ntp-4.2.6p5-19.el7.centos.1.x86_64                          1/3
  Verifying  : autogen-libopts-5.18-5.el7.x86_64                           2/3
  Verifying  : ntpdate-4.2.6p5-19.el7.centos.1.x86_64                      3/3

Removed:
  autogen-libopts.x86_64 0:5.18-5.el7          ntp.x86_64 0:4.2.6p5-19.el7.centos.1
  ntpdate.x86_64 0:4.2.6p5-19.el7.centos.1

Complete!
~]#
```

Now, you can redo a specific transaction using the following:

```
~]# yum history redo 7
```

This command will reperform a specific transaction (as defined by the transaction ID), as follows:

```
~]# yum history redo 7
Loaded plugins: fastestmirror
Repeating transaction 7, from Sun Sep  6 00:38:46 2015
    Dep-Install autogen-libopts-5.18-5.el7.x86_64      @base
    Install      ntp-4.2.6p5-19.el7.centos.1.x86_64     @updates
    Dep-Install ntpdate-4.2.6p5-19.el7.centos.1.x86_64 @updates
Loading mirror speeds from cached hostfile
 * base: ftp.belnet.be
 * epel: epel.mirror.nucleus.be
 * extras: ftp.belnet.be
 * updates: ftp.belnet.be
Resolving Dependencies
--> Running transaction check
---> Package ntp.x86_64 0:4.2.6p5-19.el7.centos.1 will be installed
--> Processing Dependency: ntpdate = 4.2.6p5-19.el7.centos.1 for package: ntp-4.2.6p5-19.el7.centos.1.
x86_64
--> Processing Dependency: libopts.so.25()(64bit) for package: ntp-4.2.6p5-19.el7.centos.1.x86_64
--> Running transaction check
---> Package autogen-libopts.x86_64 0:5.18-5.el7 will be installed
---> Package ntpdate.x86_64 0:4.2.6p5-19.el7.centos.1 will be installed
--> Finished Dependency Resolution

Dependencies Resolved

================================================================================
 Package            Arch         Version                    Repository     Size
================================================================================
Installing:
 ntp                x86_64       4.2.6p5-19.el7.centos.1    updates        540 k
Installing for dependencies:
 autogen-libopts    x86_64       5.18-5.el7                 base            66 k
 ntpdate            x86_64       4.2.6p5-19.el7.centos.1    updates         82 k

Transaction Summary
================================================================================
Install  1 Package (+2 Dependent packages)

Total download size: 689 k
Installed size: 1.6 M
Is this ok [y/d/N]: y
Downloading packages:
(1/3): autogen-libopts-5.18-5.el7.x86_64.rpm            |  66 kB  00:00:00
(2/3): ntpdate-4.2.6p5-19.el7.centos.1.x86_64.rpm       |  82 kB  00:00:00
(3/3): ntp-4.2.6p5-19.el7.centos.1.x86_64.rpm           | 540 kB  00:00:00
--------------------------------------------------------------------------------
Total                                          540 kB/s | 689 kB  00:00:01
Running transaction check
Running transaction test
Transaction test succeeded
Running transaction
  Installing : autogen-libopts-5.18-5.el7.x86_64                        1/3
  Installing : ntpdate-4.2.6p5-19.el7.centos.1.x86_64                   2/3
  Installing : ntp-4.2.6p5-19.el7.centos.1.x86_64                       3/3
  Verifying  : ntp-4.2.6p5-19.el7.centos.1.x86_64                       1/3
  Verifying  : ntpdate-4.2.6p5-19.el7.centos.1.x86_64                   2/3
  Verifying  : autogen-libopts-5.18-5.el7.x86_64                        3/3

Installed:
  ntp.x86_64 0:4.2.6p5-19.el7.centos.1

Dependency Installed:
  autogen-libopts.x86_64 0:5.18-5.el7        ntpdate.x86_64 0:4.2.6p5-19.el7.centos.1

Complete!
~]#
```

Roll back to a certain point in your transaction history

This allows you to undo all transactions up until the transaction ID that you specify. Run the following command:

```
~]# yum history rollback 6
```

Here, the transaction ID up to which you roll back is 6. You will get the following output:

```
~]# yum history rollback 6
Loaded plugins: fastestmirror
Rollback to transaction 6, from Sat Sep  5 15:53:49 2015
  Undoing the following transactions: 7, 8, 9
    Dep-Install autogen-libopts-5.18-5.el7.x86_64      @base
    Install     ntp-4.2.6p5-19.el7.centos.1.x86_64     @updates
    Dep-Install ntpdate-4.2.6p5-19.el7.centos.1.x86_64 @updates
Resolving Dependencies
--> Running transaction check
---> Package autogen-libopts.x86_64 0:5.18-5.el7 will be erased
---> Package ntp.x86_64 0:4.2.6p5-19.el7.centos.1 will be erased
---> Package ntpdate.x86_64 0:4.2.6p5-19.el7.centos.1 will be erased
--> Finished Dependency Resolution

Dependencies Resolved

================================================================================
 Package          Arch        Version                    Repository       Size
================================================================================
Removing:
 autogen-libopts  x86_64      5.18-5.el7                 @base           142 k
 ntp              x86_64      4.2.6p5-19.el7.centos.1    @updates        1.4 M
 ntpdate          x86_64      4.2.6p5-19.el7.centos.1    @updates        121 k

Transaction Summary
================================================================================
Remove  3 Packages

Installed size: 1.6 M
Is this ok [y/N]: y
Downloading packages:
Running transaction check
Running transaction test
Transaction test succeeded
Running transaction
  Erasing    : ntp-4.2.6p5-19.el7.centos.1.x86_64                         1/3
warning: file /etc/ntp.conf: remove failed: No such file or directory
  Erasing    : autogen-libopts-5.18-5.el7.x86_64                          2/3
  Erasing    : ntpdate-4.2.6p5-19.el7.centos.1.x86_64                     3/3
  Verifying  : ntp-4.2.6p5-19.el7.centos.1.x86_64                         1/3
  Verifying  : autogen-libopts-5.18-5.el7.x86_64                          2/3
  Verifying  : ntpdate-4.2.6p5-19.el7.centos.1.x86_64                     3/3

Removed:
  autogen-libopts.x86_64 0:5.18-5.el7         ntp.x86_64 0:4.2.6p5-19.el7.centos.1
  ntpdate.x86_64 0:4.2.6p5-19.el7.centos.1

Complete!
~]#
```

There's more...

You have to be careful when you use history options such as undo and rollback. Yum does its best to comply, but it cannot restore configurations, and it will not restore previous versions of your configuration files if you have edited them. This is not a fail-safe option if you don't have any backups. Although both options are very useful, I recommend that you do not use them too often. When you do use them, try to keep the impact of the transactions as small as possible. The smaller the delta, the more chance of succeeding in undoing or rolling back!

See also

Refer to the *yum(8)* man pages for more information about yum history options.

Creating a copy of an RHN repository

In this recipe, I'll show you how you can set up a yum repository for Red Hat Network-based and "plain" yum repositories.

Getting ready

Before you create a copy of an RHN repository, you need to ensure that you have a valid subscription to the repository that you want to duplicate. When this prerequisite is met, you can perform this recipe from the machine that uses the subscription.

How to do it...

Before being able to create yum repositories, we need to install a couple of tools by performing the following steps:

1. Install the `createrepo` and `yum-utils` packages using the following command:

   ```
   ~]# yum install -y yum-utils createrepo
   ```

2. Now, install the Apache web server, as follows:

   ```
   ~]# yum install -y httpd
   ```

Syncing RHN repositories

You can only sync RHN subscriptions that you have access to. Perform the following steps:

1. Create a directory to hold the RHN `rhel7` repository, as follows:

   ```
   ~]# mkdir /var/www/html/repo/rhel/rhel-x86_64-server-7/packages
   ```

2. Now, create `/mnt/iso` by executing the following command:

```
~]# mkdir -p /mnt/iso
```

3. Mount the RHEL 7 Server DVD through the following:

```
~]# mount -o loop,ro /tmp/rhel-server-7.0-x86_64-dvd.iso /mnt/iso
```

4. Now, copy the `*-comps-Server.x86_64.xml` file from the RHEL Server DVD to your `repo` directory. The following command will help in this:

```
~]# cp /mnt/iso/repodata/*-comps-Server.x86_64.xml /var/www/html/repo/rhel/comps-Server.x86_64.xml
```

5. Unmount the RHEL Server DVD, as follows:

```
~]# umount /mnt/iso
```

6. Synchronize the RHEL 7 OS repository by running the following command: (This may take a while... I suggest you kill time drinking a cup of freshly ground Arabica coffee!)

```
~]# reposync --repoid=rhel-7-server-rpms --norepopath –download_path=/var/www/html/repo/rhel/rhel-x86_64-server-7/packages
```

7. Next, create the local repository (depending on your hardware, this may take a long time), as follows:

```
~]# cd /var/www/html/repo/rhel/rhel-x86_64-server-7/
```

```
~]# createrepo --groupfile=/var/www/html/repo/rhel/comps-Server.x86_64.xml .
```

8. Finally, test your repository through the following:

```
~]# curl http://localhost/repo/rhel/rhel-x86_64-server-7/repodata/repomd.xml
```

Let's create a copy of the EPEL repository through the following steps:

1. First, install the EPEL repository, as follows:

```
~]# yum install -y epel-release
```

2. Create a directory to hold the EPEL repository by executing the following command:

```
~]# mkdir -p /var/www/html/repo/epel/7/x86_64
```

3. Now, download the `*-comps-epel7.xml` file to `/repo` as `comps-epel7.xml`, as follows:

```
~]# curl -o /var/www/html/repo/epel/comps-epel7.xml http://mirror.kinamo.be/epel/7/x86_64/repodata/xxxxxxxxxxxxxxxxxxxxx-comps-epel7.xml
```

You will need to replace the multiple x's with the correct MD5 hash, as found in the `repodata` folder.

1. Next, synchronize the EPEL repository by executing the following (this may take a very long time, depending on your hardware and internet speed):

   ```
   ~]# reposync --repoid=epel --norepopath –download_path=/var/www/
   html/repo/epel/7/x86_64
   ```

2. Create the local repository (again, depending on your hardware, this may take a long time), as follows:

   ```
   ~]# cd /var/www/html/repo/epel/7/x86_64
   ```

   ```
   ~]# createrepo --groupfile=/var/www/html/repo/epel/comps-epel7.xml
   .
   ```

3. Finally, test your repository by executing the following command:

   ```
   ~]# curl http://localhost/repo/epel/7/x86_64/repodata/repomd.xml
   ```

There's more...

When synchronizing RHEL 7 repositories, you will only be able to sync those you have entitlement to. To find out what entitlements you have on a given system connected to RHN, execute the following:

```
~]# cd /etc/yum/pluginconf.d/ && echo *.conf | sed "s/rhnplugin.
conf//"|sed 's/\([0-9a-zA-Z\-]*\).conf/--disableplugin=\1/g'|xargs yum
repolist && cd - >/dev/null
```

Whenever you synchronize a repository, try to keep the same directory structure as the original. I have found that it makes life easier when you want to rewrite your `/etc/yum.repos.d` files.

In an enterprise, it is useful to have a point in time when you "freeze" your yum repositories to ensure that all your systems are at the same RPM level. By default, any repository is "live" and gets updated whenever a new package is added. The advantage of this is that you always have the latest version of all packages available; the downside is that your environment is not uniform and you can end up troubleshooting for different versions of the same package.

The easiest way to achieve a "frozen" repository is to create a central location that holds all the RPMs as you would a normal yum mirror or copy.

Every x time, which you predefine, create a new directory with a timestamp, in which you hard link all the RPMs you mirror. Then finally, create a hard link to the directory, which you will later use in your repo configuration.

Here's an example:

Directories	Description
`/rhel7/x86_64.all`	This directory contains a mirror which is synced nightly. RPMs are added, never deleted.
`/rhel7/x86_64.20150701`	This directory contains hard links to the RPMs in `/rhel7/x86_64`, all of which were synced on 01/07/2015, along with monthly iterations of the `/rhel6/x86_64.20150701` directory.
`/rhel7/x86_64`	This directory contains a hard link to the monthly iteration, which is deemed in production.

Of course, you need to ensure that you create a repository for each new sync!

See also

Refer to the *createrepo(8)* man pages for more information about creating a repository.

Also, refer to the *reposync(1)* man pages for more information on keeping your repository up-to-date.

Configuring additional repositories

Whether you create your own mirror repository or organizations provide software for you in repositories, setting up additional repositories on your RHEL system is quite simple. This recipe will show you how to set them up. Many repositories have their own repo files or even an RPM that automatically installs the repository. When these are available, don't hesitate to use them!

Getting ready

For this to work, you will need to have a repository set up, which can be accessed through the following URL: `http://repo.example.com/myrepo/7/x86_64`.

How to do it...

In order to create an additional repository, create a file in `/etc/yum.repos.d` called `myrepo.repo`, which contains the following information:

```
[myrepo]
name=My Personal Repository
baseurl=http://repo.example.com/myrepo/$releasever/$basearch
gpgcheck=0
enabled=1
```

There's more...

The `gpgcheck=1` option only functions if you or the provider of a repo has signed all the RPMs in the repo. This is generally a good practice and provides extra security to your repositories.

The `$releasever` and `$basearch` variables allow you to create a single repository file that can work on multiple systems as long as you have a repository for the URLs. The `$releasever` variable expands to the major version of the OS (7 in our case), and the `$basearch` will expands to x86_64. On an i386 system (RHEL 7 only comes in the x86_64 architecture), `$basearch` expands to i386.

You can find many repositories on the Internet, such as `epel` and `elrepo`, but it may not always be a good idea to use them. Any software provided by the Red Hat standard repositories are also supported by Red Hat, and they will no longer support you if you start using the same software provided through another repository. So, you better ensure that you don't care about support or have another party that is willing to support you.

See also

Although I do not condone the use of these in production without taking the appropriate support actions, here is a list of some popular repositories that you can use:

The ELRepo repository can be found at:

`http://elrepo.org/tiki/tiki-index.php`

The EPEL repository is at:

`https://fedoraproject.org/wiki/EPEL`

The Puppetlabs repositories can be found at:

`https://docs.puppetlabs.com/guides/puppetlabs_package_repositories.html`

The Zabbix repositories are at the following link:

`https://www.zabbix.com/documentation/2.0/manual/installation/install_from_packages`

For the RepoForge repositories, refer to the following website:

`http://repoforge.org/use/`

Remi's repositories can be found at:

`http://rpms.famillecollet.com/`

The Webtatic repositories are at:

```
https://webtatic.com/projects/yum-repository/
```

Setting up yum to automatically update

In enterprises, automating the systematic updating of your RHEL systems is very important. You want to stay ahead of hackers or, in general, people trying to hurt you by exploiting the weaknesses in your environment.

Although I do not recommend applying this recipe to all systems in an enterprise, this is quite useful to ensure that certain systems are kept up to date as the patches and bugfixes are applied to the RPMs in Red Hat's (and other) repositories.

Getting ready

In order for this recipe to work, you'll need to be sure that the repositories you are using are set up correctly and you have valid mail setup (using Postfix or Sendmail, for example).

How to do it...

We'll set up yum to autoupdate your system once a week (at 03:00) and reboot if necessary through the following steps:

1. Install the yum cron plugin, as follows:

    ```
    ~]# yum install -y yum-cron
    ```

2. Then, disable the hourly and daily yum cron jobs through the following commands:

    ```
    ~]# echo > /etc/cron.dhourly/0yum-hourly.cron
    ~]# echo > /etc/cron.daily/0yum-daily.cron
    ```

3. Create the configuration file for the weekly yum update cron job via the following:

    ```
    ~]# cp /etc/yum/yum-cron.conf /etc/yum/yum-cron-weekly.conf
    ```

4. Modify the created configuration file to apply updates and send a notification through e-mail by setting the following values:

    ```
    apply_updates = yes
    emit_via = email
    email_to = <your email address>
    ```

5. Next, create a weekly cron job by adding the following contents to `/etc/cron.weekly/yum-weekly.cron`:

```bash
#!/bin/bash


# Only run if this flag is set. The flag is created by the yum-
cron init
# script when the service is started -- this allows one to use
chkconfig and
# the standard "service stop|start" commands to enable or disable
yum-cron.
if [[ ! -f /var/lock/subsys/yum-cron ]]; then
   exit 0
fi


# Action!
exec /usr/sbin/yum-cron /etc/yum/yum-cron-weekly.conf
if test "$(yum history info |egrep '\skernel'|wc -l)" != "0"; then
    /sbin/shutdown --reboot +5 "Kernel has been upgraded,
rebooting the server in 5 minutes. Please save your work."
fi
```

6. Finally, make the cron job executable by executing the following command:

```
~]# chmod +x /etc/cron.weekly/yum-weekly.cron
```

How it works...

By default, `yum-cron` sets up a cron job that is run every hour (`/etc/cron.dhourly/0yum-hourly.cron`) and every day (`/etc/cron.daily/0yum-daily.cron`).

There's more...

This recipe will upgrade all your packages when there's an update available. If you just want to apply security fixes, modify the `update_cmd` value of your yum cron configuration file in the following way:

```
update_cmd = security
```

Alternatively, you can even use the following configuration if you only want critical fixes:

```
update_cmd = security-severity:Critical
```

See also

Check the *yum cron(8)* man page or the default `yum-cron.conf` file located at `/etc/yum/yum-cron.conf` for more information.

Configuring logrotate for yum

Every time you use yum to install and/or update packages, it logs to `/var/log/yum.log`. A lot of people don't want to rotate the file a lot as they believe (incorrectly) that it is their only source to the history of their yum tasks. They may even believe that it provides a way to restore your rpm database if it gets corrupted - it does not.

I do recommend keeping your complete yum history as it doesn't grow a lot, unless you reinstall packages a lot.

For a rich interface to your yum history, I suggest you use yum history.

By default, your yum log file is rotated yearly, and even then, it only rotates if the size of your log file exceeds 30 KB, and your logs are only kept for 4 years. Usually, this is enough in the physical world as physical servers tend to be replaced every 3-4 years. However, virtual servers have the potential to stay "alive" beyond these 3-4 years.

How to do it...

Modify `/etc/logrotate.d/yum` to the following:

```
/var/log/yum.log {
    missingok
    notifempty
    size 30k
    rotate 1000
    yearly
    create 0600  root  root
}
```

How it works...

This configuration will only rotate the yum log when it exceeds 30 KB in size on a yearly basis, and it will keep 1000 rotated logs, which is basically log files for 1000 years!

See also

For more information on how to use and configure logrotate, refer to the *logrotate(8)* man page.

Recovering from a corrupted RPM database

Although everything is done to ensure that your RPM databases are intact, your RPM database may become corrupt and unuseable. This happens mainly if the filesystem on which the rpm db resides is suddenly inaccessible (full, read-only, reboot, or so on).

This recipe will show you the two ways in which you can attempt to restore your RPM database.

Getting ready

Verify that your system is backed up in some way.

How to do it...

We'll start with the easiest option and the one with the highest success rate in these steps:

1. Start by creating a backup of your corrupt rpm db, as follows:

    ```
    ~]# cd; tar zcvf rpm-db.tar.gz /var/lib/rpm/*
    ```

2. Remove stale lock files if they exist through the following command:

    ```
    ~]# rm -f /var/lib/rpm/__db*
    ```

3. Now, verify the integrity of the Packages database via the following:

    ```
    ~]# /usr/lib/rpm/rpmdb_verify /var/lib/rpm/Packages; echo $?
    ```

    If the previous step prints 0, proceed to Step 7.

4. Rename the Packages file (don't delete it, we'll need it!), as follows:

    ```
    ~]# mv /var/lib/rpm/Packages  /var/lib/rpm/Packages.org
    ```

5. Now, dump the Packages db from the original Packages db by executing the following command:

    ```
    ~]# cd /usr/lib/rpm/rpmdb_dump Packages.org | /usr/lib/rpm/rpmdb_
    load Packages
    ```

6. Verify the integrity of the newly created Packages database. Run the following:

    ```
    ~]# /usr/lib/rpm/rpmdb_verify /var/lib/rpm/Packages; echo $?
    ```

    If the exit code is not 0, you will need to restore the database from backup.

7. Rebuild the `rpm` indexes, as follows:

   ```
   ~]# rpm -vv --rebuilddb
   ```

8. Next, use the following command to check the `rpm  db` with yum for any other issues (this may take a long time):

   ```
   ~]# yum check
   ```

9. Restore the SELinux context of the `rpm` database through the following command:

   ```
   ~]# restorecon -R -v /var/lib/rpm
   ```

```
~]# tar zcvf rpm-db.tar.gz /var/lib/rpm/*
tar: Removing leading '/' from member names
/var/lib/rpm/Basenames
/var/lib/rpm/Conflictname
/var/lib/rpm/Dirnames
/var/lib/rpm/Group
/var/lib/rpm/Installtid
/var/lib/rpm/Name
/var/lib/rpm/Obsoletename
/var/lib/rpm/Packages
/var/lib/rpm/Providename
/var/lib/rpm/Requirename
/var/lib/rpm/Shalheader
/var/lib/rpm/Sigmd5
/var/lib/rpm/Triggername
~]# rm -f /var/lib/rpm/__db*
~]# /usr/lib/rpm/rpmdb_verify /var/lib/rpm/Packages; echo $?
BDB5105 Verification of /var/lib/rpm/Packages succeeded.
0
~]# rpm -vv --rebuilddb
D: rebuilding database /var/lib/rpm into /var/lib/rpmrebuilddb.13427
D: opening  db environment /var/lib/rpm private:0x401
D: opening  db index       /var/lib/rpm/Packages 0x400 mode=0x0
D: locked   db index       /var/lib/rpm/Packages
D: opening  db environment /var/lib/rpmrebuilddb.13427 private:0x401
D: opening  db index       /var/lib/rpmrebuilddb.13427/Packages (none) mode=0x42
D: opening  db index       /var/lib/rpmrebuilddb.13427/Packages 0x1 mode=0x42

...

D: adding 1 entries to Installtid index.
D: adding 1 entries to Sigmd5 index.
D: adding "22f5db5a1d2a3be92a0457d47020c1fb0baa22b0" to Shalheader index.
D: closed   db index       /var/lib/rpm/Packages
D: closed   db environment /var/lib/rpm
D: closed   db index       /var/lib/rpmrebuilddb.13427/Shalheader
D: closed   db index       /var/lib/rpmrebuilddb.13427/Sigmd5
D: closed   db index       /var/lib/rpmrebuilddb.13427/Installtid
D: closed   db index       /var/lib/rpmrebuilddb.13427/Dirnames
D: closed   db index       /var/lib/rpmrebuilddb.13427/Triggername
D: closed   db index       /var/lib/rpmrebuilddb.13427/Obsoletename
D: closed   db index       /var/lib/rpmrebuilddb.13427/Conflictname
D: closed   db index       /var/lib/rpmrebuilddb.13427/Providename
D: closed   db index       /var/lib/rpmrebuilddb.13427/Requirename
D: closed   db index       /var/lib/rpmrebuilddb.13427/Group
D: closed   db index       /var/lib/rpmrebuilddb.13427/Basenames
D: closed   db index       /var/lib/rpmrebuilddb.13427/Name
D: closed   db index       /var/lib/rpmrebuilddb.13427/Packages
D: closed   db environment /var/lib/rpmrebuilddb.13427
~]#
```

There's more...

If, for some reason, you are unable to recover your RPM database, there is one final option left. Enterprises tend to have standardized builds, and many servers are installed with the same packages, so copy the healthy `/var/lib/rpm` directory from another server with the exact same package set to the corrupted one, and perform the preceding recipe's steps to ensure that everything is okay.

Although you'll find additional tools that can save your skin (such as RPM cron), it's usually more practical to have a decent backup.

9
Securing RHEL 7

In this chapter, you will learn all about:

- ▶ Installing and configuring IPA
- ▶ Securing the system login
- ▶ Configuring privilege escalation with sudo
- ▶ Securing the network with `firewalld`
- ▶ Using kdump and SysRq
- ▶ Using ABRT
- ▶ Auditing the system

Introduction

Security is an important aspect of your environment. The recipes provided in this chapter are not a definitive set of how-tos; rather, they are a start to addressing security in an environment as every environment is different. This chapter is meant to give you an idea of what you can do with a simple set of tools included in Red Hat Enterprise Server 7.

In this chapter, I will not attempt explaining where the system stores syslog messages and what they mean as this can be quite an exhaustive topic. The most important security-related syslog messages can be found in `/var/log/secure` and `/var/log/audit/audit.log`.

Installing and configuring IPA

The **IPA** (**Identity Policy Audit**) server allows you to manage your kerberos, DNS, hosts, users, sudo rules, password policies, and automounts in a central location. IPA is a combination of packages, including—but not limited to—bind, ldap, pam, and so on. It combines all of these to provide identity management for your environment.

Getting ready

In this recipe, I will opt for an integrated DNS setup, although it is possible to use your existing DNS infrastructure.

How to do it...

First, we'll install the server component, followed by what needs to be done on an IPA client.

Installing the IPA server

Follow these instructions to install an IPA server:

1. Install the necessary packages via the following command:

    ```
    ~]# yum install -y ipa-server bind bind-dyndb-ldap
    ```

2. When the packages are installed, invoke the ipa installer, as follows:

    ```
    ~]# ipa-server-install
    ```

At this stage, you will be asked a couple of questions on how to set up your IPA server.

1. Configure integrated DNS as follows:

    ```
    Do you want to configure integrated DNS (BIND)? [no]: yes
    ```

2. Overwrite existing /etc/resolv.conf as follows:

    ```
    Existing BIND configuration detected, overwrite? [no]: yes
    ```

3. Provide the IPA server's hostname, as follows:

    ```
    Server host name [localhost.localdomain]: master.example.com
    ```

4. Now, confirm the DNS domain name for the IPA server as follows:

    ```
    Please confirm the domain name [example.com]:
    ```

5. Provide an IP address for the IPA server as follows:

   ```
   Please provide the IP address to be used for this host name:
   192.168.0.1
   ```

6. Next, provide a Kerberos `realm` name, as follows:

   ```
   Please provide a realm name [EXAMPLE.COM]:
   ```

7. Create the directory manager's password and confirm it as follows:

   ```
   Directory Manager password:
   ```

8. Create the IPA manager's password and confirm it as follows:

   ```
   IPA admin password:
   ```

9. Now, configure the DNS forwarders as follows:

   ```
   Do you want to configure DNS forwarders? [yes]: no
   ```

10. Finally, configure the reverse DNS zones as follows:

    ```
    Do you want to configure the reverse zone? [yes]:
    Please specify the reverse zone name [0.168.192.in-addr.arpa.]:
    ```

    The installer will now provide an overview similar to the following:

    ```
    The IPA Master Server will be configured with:
    Hostname:       master.example.com
    IP address:     192.168.0.1
    Domain name:    example.com
    Realm name:     EXAMPLE.COM


    BIND DNS server will be configured to serve IPA domain with:
    Forwarders:     No forwarders
    Reverse zone:   0.168.192.in-addr.arpa.
    ```

11. Now, confirm the information by typing "yes", as follows:

    ```
    Continue to configure the system with these values? [no]: yes
    ```

At this point, you will see a lot of information scrolling on your screen, indicating what the installer is doing: installing or configuring NTP, LDAP, BIND, Kerberos, HTTP, the certificate server, and IPA-related modifications to the preceding examples.

The installation and configuration process can take a while, so be patient.

Installing the IPA client

Perform these steps to install and configure the IPA client on your system:

 Ensure that the hostname of your system is different from `localhost.localdomain`. If it is not, the client configuration will fail.

1. Install the necessary packages via the following command:

    ```
    ~]# yum install -y ipa-client
    ```

2. Ensure that the IPA server is used as a DNS server through the following:

    ```
    ~]# cat /etc/resolv.conf

    search example.com

    nameserver 192.168.0.1
    ```

3. Invoke the IPA client configuration by running this command line:

    ```
    ~]# ipa-client-install --enable-dns-updates
    ```

The installer will now show an overview of the detected IPA server and ask for a user (the IPA manager) and password to register your system, as shown in the following screenshot:

```
~]# ipa-client-install --enable-dns-updates
Discovery was successful!
Hostname: guest.example.com
Realm: EXAMPLE.COM
DNS Domain: example.com
IPA Server: master.example.com
BaseDN: dc=example,dc=com

Continue to configure the system with these values? [no]: yes
User authorized to enroll computers: admin
Synchronizing time with KDC...
Password for admin@EXAMPLE.COM:
Successfully retrieved CA cert
    Subject:    CN=Certificate Authority,O=EXAMPLE.COM
    Issuer:     CN=Certificate Authority,O=EXAMPLE.COM
    Valid From: Fri Oct 30 13:40:04 2015 UTC
    Valid Until: Tue Oct 30 13:40:04 2035 UTC

Enrolled in IPA realm EXAMPLE.COM
Created /etc/ipa/default.conf
New SSSD config will be created
Configured /etc/sssd/sssd.conf
Configured /etc/krb5.conf for IPA realm EXAMPLE.COM
trying https://master.example.com/ipa/xml
Forwarding 'ping' to server 'https://master.example.com/ipa/xml'
Forwarding 'env' to server 'https://master.example.com/ipa/xml'
Hostname (guest.example.com) not found in DNS
DNS server record set to: guest.example.com -> 192.168.0.2
Adding SSH public key from /etc/ssh/ssh_host_rsa_key.pub
Adding SSH public key from /etc/ssh/ssh_host_ecdsa_key.pub
Forwarding 'host_mod' to server 'https://master.example.com/ipa/xml'
SSSD enabled
Configured /etc/openldap/ldap.conf
NTP enabled
Configured /etc/ssh/ssh_config
Configured /etc/ssh/sshd_config
Client configuration complete.
~]#
```

There's more...

Once installed, you can manage your IPA environment using the command line tool IPA or the web interface, which can be accessed by pointing your browser to your IPA master server over HTTPS. In this case, the URL is `https://master.example.com`.

By default, the IPA client doesn't create `homedirs` for new users at first login. If you want to enable this, use the `--mkhomedir` argument with `ipa-client-install`. If you happen to have forgotten about this, there's no need to reinstall the IPA client. You can just reconfigure this by executing the following command:

```
~]# authconfig --enablemkhomedir --update
```

See also

For more in-depth information about installing and configuring your IPA server, go to `https://access.redhat.com/documentation/en-US/Red_Hat_Enterprise_Linux/7/html/Linux_Domain_Identity_Authentication_and_Policy_Guide/installing-ipa.html`.

For more information about managing your IPA environment through the command line, read the *ipa (1)* man pages.

Securing the system login

The default settings applied to system login are based on what Red Hat deems basic security. If, for some reason, you want to change this, this recipe will show you a couple of examples. Authconfig has two tools that you can use to configure authentication: `authconfig` and `authconfig-tui`.

These two tools configure `pam` for you in such a way that the changes are consistent throughout rpm updates.

The `authconfig-tui` tool is not as feature-rich as the plan `authconfig` tool, which I personally recommend you to use as it allows you to do more.

You can manually edit the files located in `/etc/pam.d` if and when you know what you're doing, but this is not recommended.

How to do it...

Perform the following steps:

First, change the hash encryption of the passwords stored in `/etc/shadow` to `sha512`, as follows:

```
~]# authconfig --passalgo=sha512 --update
```

Enable NIS authentication through the following command:

```
~]# authconfig --enablenis –nisdomain=NISDOMAIN --nisserver=nisserver.
example.com --update
```

Now, set the minimum length requirement for passwords to `16` via the following:

```
~]# authconfig --passminlen=16 --update
```

The user requires at least one lowercase letter in the password; you can set this requirement by running the following:

```
~]# authconfig --enablereqlower --update
```

Also, the user requires at least one uppercase letter in the password, for which you can run the following:

```
~]# authconfig --enablerequpper --update
```

Now, the user requires at least one number in the password. Execute the following command for this:

```
~]# authconfig --enablereqdigit --update
```

Finally, the user requires at least one nonalphanumeric character in the password, which you can set using the following command:

```
~]# authconfig --enablereqother --update
```

How it works...

`authconfig` and `authconfig-tui` are wrapper scripts that modify a variety of files, including, but not limited to, `/etc/nsswitch.conf`, `/etc/pam.d/*`, `/etc/sssd.conf`, `/etc/openldap/ldap.conf`, and `/etc/sysconfig/network`.

The advantage of the tool is that it uses the correct syntax, which can sometimes be a little tricky, especially for the files in `/etc/pam.d`.

There's more...

One of the interesting features of this tool is the backup and restore functions. In case you do not use any centralized identification and authentication infrastructure, such as IPA, you can use this to make a backup of a correctly configured machine and distribute this through whichever means you wish to use.

To back up your `authconf` configuration, execute the following:

```
~]# authconfig --savebackup=/tmp/auth.conf
```

This will create a `/tmp/auth.conf` directory, which contains all the files modified by `authconfig`.

Copy this directory over to another server and restore the configuration by executing the following:

```
~]# authconfig --restorebackup=/tmp/auth.conf
```

All of the security changes you apply through `authconfig` can also be managed through IPA.

See also

For information about and more configuration options, take a look at the *authconfig (8)* man pages.

You can also find more information on Red Hat's page on authentication at `https://access.redhat.com/documentation/en-US/Red_Hat_Enterprise_Linux/7/html/System-Level_Authentication_Guide/Configuring_Authentication.html`.

Configuring privilege escalation with sudo

Sudo allows users to run applications and scripts with the security privileges of another user.

Getting ready

Before allowing someone to elevate their security context for a specific application or script, you need to figure out which user or group you wish to elevate from and to, which applications/scripts you use, and on which systems to run them.

The default syntax for a sudo entry is the following:

```
who where = (as_whom) what
```

How to do it...

These simple five steps will guide you through setting up privilege escalation:

1. Create a new `sudoers` definition file in `/etc/sudoers.d/` called clustering through the following command:

   `~]# visudo -f /etc/sudoers.d/clustering`

2. Create a command alias for the most-used clustering tools called CLUSTERING by executing the following:

   `Cmnd_Alias CLUSTERING = /sbin/ccs, /sbin/clustat, /sbin/clusvcadm`

3. Now, create a host alias group for all the clusters called CLUSTERS, as follows:

   `Host_Alias CLUSTERS = cluster1, cluster2`

4. Next, create a user alias for all cluster admins called CLUSTERADMINS by executing the following:

   `User_Alias CLUSTERADMINS = spalpatine, dvader, okenobi, qjinn`

5. Now, let's create a sudo rule that allows the users from CLUSTERADMINS to execute commands from CLUSTERING on all servers within the CLUSTERS group, as follows:

   `CLUSTERADMINS CLUSTERS = (root) CLUSTERING`

There's more...

To edit the `sudoers` file, you can either use a text editor and edit `/etc/sudoers`, the `visudo` tool, which automatically checks your syntax when exiting.

It's always a good idea to leave the original `/etc/sudoers` file alone and modify the files located in `/etc/sudoers.d/`. This allows the sudo rpm to update the `sudoers` file should it be necessary.

See also

For more information about sudo, take a look at the *sudoers (5)* man page.

Secure the network with firewalld

`firewalld` is a set of scripts and a daemon that manage `netfilter` on your RHEL system. It aims at creating a simple command-line interface to manage the firewall on your systems.

How to do it...

By default, `firewalld` is included in the "core" rpm group, but it may not be installed for some reason (that you left it out of your kickstart would be one!). Perform the following steps:

1. Install `firewalld` via the following command line:

   ```
   ~]# yum install -y firewalld
   ```

2. Now, enable `firewalld` through the following:

   ```
   ~]# systemctl enable firewalld
   ```

3. Finally, ensure that `firewalld` is started by executing the following command line:

   ```
   ~]# systemctl restart firewalld
   ```

Showing the currently allowed services and ports on your system

List all the allowed services using the following command:

```
~]# firewall-cmd –list-services
```

You can see the output as follows, where all the allowed services are listed:

```
~]# firewall-cmd --list-services
dhcpv6-client http https ssh
~]#
```

Now, show the `tcp/udp` ports that are allowed by your firewall using the following command:

```
~]# firewall-cmd --list-ports
```

Here's what the output should look like:

```
~]# firewall-cmd --list-ports
~]# []
```

Allowing incoming requests for NFS (v4)

Perform the following steps to allow NFSv4 traffic on your system:

1. First, allow nfs traffic via this command:

   ```
   ~]# firewall-cmd --add-service nfs --permanent
   success
   ~]#
   ```

2. Then, reload the configuration as follows:

   ```
   ~]# firewall-cmd --reload
   success
   ~]#
   ```

3. Now, check the newly applied rule by executing the following command line:

   ```
   ~]# firewall-cmd --list-services
   nfs
   ~]#
   ```

Allowing incoming requests on an arbitrary port

Perform the following steps to allow incoming traffic on port 1234 over both tcp and udp:

1. First, allow traffic on port 1234 over tcp and udp by running the following:

   ```
   ~]# firewall-cmd --add-port 1234/tcp --permanent
   success
   ~]# firewall-cmd --add-port 1234/udp --permanent
   success
   ~]#
   ```

2. Reload the configuration by executing the following command:

    ```
    ~]# firewall-cmd --reload
    success
    ~]#
    ```

3. Check the newly applied rule via the following:

    ```
    ~]# firewall-cmd --list-ports
    1234/tcp 1234/udp
    ~]#
    ```

There's more...

`firewalld` comes with a set of predefined port configurations, such as HTTP and HTTPS. You can find all such definitions in `/lib/firewalld/services`. When creating your own port definitions or modifying the existing ones, you should create new port definition files in `/etc/firewalld/services`.

When creating new "rules" by adding ports, services, and so on, you need to add the `--permanent` option, or your changes would be lost upon the rebooting of the system or the reloading of the `firewalld` policy.

See also

For more information on configuring your firewall, check the man pages for *firewall-cmd(1)*.

Using kdump and SysRq

The kdump mechanism is a Linux kernel feature, which allows you to create dumps if your kernel crashes. It produces an exact copy of the memory, which can be analyzed for the root cause of the crash.

SysRq is a feature supported by the Linux kernel, which allows you to send key combinations to it even when your system becomes unresponsive.

How to do it...

First, we'll set up kdump and SysRq, and afterwards, I'll show you how to use it to debug a dump.

Installing and configuring kdump and SysRq

Let's take a look at how this is installed and configured:

1. Install the necessary packages for kdump by executing the following command:

    ```
    ~]# yum install -y kexec-tools
    ```

2. Ensure that `crashkernel=auto` is present in the `GRUB_CMDLINE_LINUX` variable declaration in the `/etc/sysconfig/grub` file using this command:

    ```
    GRUB_CMDLINE_LINUX="rd.lvm.lv=system/usr
    rd.lvm.lv=system/swap vconsole.keymap=us
    rd.lvm.lv=system/root vconsole.font=latarcyrheb-sun16
    crashkernel=auto"
    ```

3. Start `kdump` by running the following:

    ```
    ~]# systemctl start kdump
    ```

4. Now, enable `kdump` to start at boot, as follows:

    ```
    ~]# sysctl enable kdump
    ```

5. Configure SysRq to accept all commands via the following commands:

    ```
    ~]# echo "kernel.sysrq = 1" >> /etc/sysctl.d/sysrq.conf
    ```

    ```
    ~]# systemctl -q -p /etc/sysctl.d/sysrq.conf
    ```

6. Regenerate your **intramfs** (**initial RAM file system**) to contain the necessary information for kdump by executing the following command:

    ```
    ~]# dracut --force
    ```

7. Finally, reboot through the following command:

    ```
    ~]# reboot
    ```

Using kdump tools to analyze the dump

Although you'll find most of the information you're looking for in the `vmcode-dmesg.txt` file, it can be useful sometimes to look into the bits and bytes of the `vmcore` dump, even if it is just to know what the people at Red Hat do when they ask you to send you a `vmcore` dump. Perform the following steps:

1. Install the necessary tools to debug the `vmcore` dump via the following command:

    ```
    ~]# yum install -y --enablerepo=\*debuginfo crash kernel-debuginfo
    ```

2. Locate your `vmcore` by executing the following:

    ```
    ~]# find /var/crash -name 'vmcore'
    /var/crash/127.0.0.1-2015.10.31-12:03:06/vmcore
    ```

If you don't have a core dump, you can trigger this yourself by executing the following:

```
~]# echo c > /proc/sysrq-trigger
```

3. Use `crash` to analyze the contents, as follows:

    ```
    ~]# crash /var/crash/127.0.0.1-2015.10.31-12:03:06/vmcore /usr/
    lib/debug/lib/modules/<kernel>/vmlinux
    ```

    Here, `<kernel>` must be the same kernel as the one that the dump was created for:

```
crash 7.0.2-6.el7
Copyright (C) 2002-2013  Red Hat, Inc.
Copyright (C) 2004, 2005, 2006, 2010  IBM Corporation
Copyright (C) 1999-2006  Hewlett-Packard Co
Copyright (C) 2005, 2006, 2011, 2012  Fujitsu Limited
Copyright (C) 2006, 2007  VA Linux Systems Japan K.K.
Copyright (C) 2005, 2011  NEC Corporation
Copyright (C) 1999, 2002, 2007  Silicon Graphics, Inc.
Copyright (C) 1999, 2000, 2001, 2002  Mission Critical Linux, Inc.
This program is free software, covered by the GNU General Public License,
and you are welcome to change it and/or distribute copies of it under
certain conditions.  Enter "help copying" to see the conditions.
This program has absolutely no warranty.  Enter "help warranty" for details.

GNU gdb (GDB) 7.6
Copyright (C) 2013 Free Software Foundation, Inc.
License GPLv3+: GNU GPL version 3 or later <http://gnu.org/licenses/gpl.html>
This is free software: you are free to change and redistribute it.
There is NO WARRANTY, to the extent permitted by law.  Type "show copying"
and "show warranty" for details.
This GDB was configured as "x86_64-unknown-linux-gnu".

      KERNEL: /usr/lib/debug/lib/modules/3.10.0-123.el7.x86_64/vmlinux
    DUMPFILE: /var/crash/127.0.0.1-2015.10.31-12:03:06/vmcore  [PARTIAL DUMP]
        CPUS: 2
        DATE: Sat Oct 31 12:03:06 2015
      UPTIME: 02:04:36
LOAD AVERAGE: 0.00, 0.01, 0.00
       TASKS: 122
    NODENAME: guest.example.com
     RELEASE: 3.10.0-123.el7.x86_64
     VERSION: #1 SMP Mon May 5 11:16:57 EDT 2014
     MACHINE: x86_64
      MEMORY: 2 GB
       PANIC: "Oops: 0002 [#1] SMP " (check log for details)
         PID: 4389
     COMMAND: "bash"
        TASK: f196d560  [THREAD_INFO: ef4da000]
         CPU: 2
       STATE: TASK_RUNNING (PANIC)

crash> 
```

4. Display the kernel message buffer (this can also be found in the `vmcore-dmesg.txt` dump file) by running the following command:

    ```
    crash> log
    ```

Here's what the output should look like:

```
crash> log
...
EIP: 0060:[<c068124f>] EFLAGS: 00010096 CPU: 2
EIP is at sysrq_handle_crash+0xf/0x20
EAX: 00000063 EBX: 00000063 ECX: c09e1c8c EDX: 00000000
ESI: c0a09ca0 EDI: 00000286 EBP: 00000000 ESP: ef4dbf24
 DS: 007b ES: 007b FS: 00d8 GS: 00a0 SS: 0068
Process bash (pid: 5591, ti=ef4da000 task=f196d560 task.ti=ef4da000)
Stack:
 c068146b c0960891 c0968653 00000003 00000002 00000002 efade5c0 c06814d0
<0> ffffffffb c068150f b7776000 f2606c40 c0569ec4 ef4dbf9c 00000602 b7776000
<0> efade5c0 00000002 b7776000 c0569e60 c051de50 ef4dbf9c f196d560 ef4dbfb4
Call Trace:
 [<c068146b>] ? __handle_sysrq+0xfb/0x160
 [<c06814d0>] ? write_sysrq_trigger+0x0/0x50
 [<c068150f>] ? write_sysrq_trigger+0x3f/0x50
 [<c0569ec4>] ? proc_reg_write+0x64/0xa0
 [<c0569e60>] ? proc_reg_write+0x0/0xa0
 [<c051de50>] ? vfs_write+0xa0/0x190
 [<c051e8d1>] ? sys_write+0x41/0x70
 [<c0409adc>] ? syscall_call+0x7/0xb
Code: a0 c0 01 0f b6 41 03 19 d2 f7 d2 83 e2 03 83 e0 cf c1 e2 04 09 d0 88 41 03 f3 c3 90 c7 05 c8 1b 9e c0 01 00 00 00
0f aa f8 89 f6 <c6> 05 00 00 00 00 01 c3 89 f6 8d bc 27 00 00 00 00 8d 50 d0 83
EIP: [<c068124f>] sysrq_handle_crash+0xf/0x20 SS:ESP 0068:ef4dbf24
CR2: 0000000000000000
crash>
```

5. Display the kernel stack trace through the following:

   ```
   crash> bt
   ```

   Here's what the output should look like:

```
crash> bt
PID: 4389   TASK: f196d560  CPU: 2   COMMAND: "bash"
 #0 [ef4dbdcc] crash_kexec at c0494922
 #1 [ef4dbe20] oops_end at c080e402
 #2 [ef4dbe34] no_context at c043089d
 #3 [ef4dbe58] bad_area at c0430b26
 #4 [ef4dbe6c] do_page_fault at c080fb9b
 #5 [ef4dbee4] error_code (via page_fault) at c080d809
    EAX: 00000063  EBX: 00000063  ECX: c09e1c8c  EDX: 00000000  EBP: 00000000
    DS:  007b      ESI: c0a09ca0  ES:  007b      EDI: 00000286  GS:  00e0
    CS:  0060      EIP: c068124f  ERR: ffffffff  EFLAGS: 00010096
 #6 [ef4dbf18] sysrq_handle_crash at c068124f
 #7 [ef4dbf24] __handle_sysrq at c0681469
 #8 [ef4dbf48] write_sysrq_trigger at c068150a
 #9 [ef4dbf54] proc_reg_write at c0569ec2
#10 [ef4dbf74] vfs_write at c051de4e
#11 [ef4dbf94] sys_write at c051e8cc
#12 [ef4dbfb0] system_call at c0409ad5
    EAX: fffffffda  EBX: 00000001  ECX: b7776000  EDX: 00000002
    DS:  007b      ESI: 00000002  ES:  007b      EDI: b7776000
    SS:  007b      ESP: bfcb2088  EBP: bfcb20b4  GS:  0033
    CS:  0073      EIP: 00edc416  ERR: 00000004  EFLAGS: 00000246
crash>
```

6. Now, show the processes at the time of the core dump, as follows:

   ```
   crash> ps
   ```

Here's what the output should look like:

```
crash> ps
   PID    PPID  CPU    TASK    ST  %MEM   VSZ    RSS  COMM
>    0      0    0  c09dc560  RU   0.0    0      0   [swapper]
>    0      0    1  f7072030  RU   0.0    0      0   [swapper]
     0      0    2  f70a3a90  RU   0.0    0      0   [swapper]
>    0      0    3  f70ac560  RU   0.0    0      0   [swapper]
     1      0    1  f705ba90  IN   0.0   2828   1424  init
...
  4221      1    1  f2592560  IN   0.0   12876   784  auditd
  4222      1    2  ef427560  IN   0.0   12876   784  auditd
  4387   4362    0  f196d030  IN   0.0   11064   3184  sshd
>  4389   4387    2  f196d560  RU   0.0   5084   1648  bash
crash> █
```

There's more...

The default kdump configuration uses `/var/crash` to dump its memory on. This MUST be on the root filesystem. Some systems are configured with a separate filesystem for `/var`, so you need to change the location in `/etc/kdump.conf` or use a different target type, such as `raw`, `nfs`, and so on. If your crash directory is located on a nonroot filesystem, the kdump service will fail!

Although the crash utility can provide a lot of details about the crash, usually you're set with the contents of the `vmcore-dmesg.txt` file, which resides in the same directory as the `vmcore` file. So, I suggest that you parse this file before digging into the bits and bytes of the memory dump.

SysRq, as stated before, allows you to control your system even if it is in a state that doesn't allow you to do anything at all. However, it does require you to have access to the system's console.

By default, kdump creates a dump and reboots your system. In the event that this doesn't happen and you don't want to push the power button on your (virtual) system, SysRq allows you to send commands through the console to your kernel.

The key combination needed to send the information differs a little from architecture to architecture. Take a look at the following table for reference:

Architecture	Key combination
x86	`<Alt><SysRq><command key>`
Sparc	`<Alt><Stop><command key>`
Serial console (PC style only)	This sends a `BREAK` and, within 5 seconds, the command key. Sending `BREAK` twice is interpreted as a normal `BREAK`.
PowerPC	`<Alt><Print Screen>`(or `<F13>`)`<command key>`

So, on an x86 system, you would attempt to sync your disks before rebooting it by executing the following commands:

`<Alt><SysRq><s>`

`<Alt><SysRq><b>`

Alternatively, if you still have access to your terminal, you can do the same by sending characters to `/proc/sysrq-trigger`, as follows:

```
~]# echo s > /proc/sysrq-trigger
~]# echo b > /proc/sysrq-trigger
```

The following key commands are available:

Command key	Function
b	This immediately reboots your system. It does not sync or unmount disks. This can result in data corruption!
c	This performs a system crash by a `NULL` pointer dereference. A crashdump is taken if kdump is configured.
d	This shows all the locks held.
e	This sends a `SIGTERM` signal to all your processes, except for `init`.
f	This calls `oom_kill` to kill any process hogging the memory.
g	This is used by the **kernel debugger** (**kgdb**).
h	This shows help. (Memorize this option!)
i	This sends a `SIGKILL` signal to all your processes, except for `init`.
j	This freezes your filesystems with the `FIFREEZE` ioctl.
k	This kills all the programs on the current virtual console. It enables a secure login from the console as this kills all malware attempting to grab your keyboard input, for example.
l	This shows a stack trace for all active CPUs.
m	This dumps the current memory info to your console.
n	You can use this to make real-time tasks niceable.
o	This shuts down your system and turns it off (if configured and supported).
p	This dumps the current registers and flags to your console
q	This will dump a list of all armed `hrtimers` (except for `timer_list` timers) per CPU together with detailed information about all clockevent devices.
r	This turns off your keyboard's raw mode and sets it to `XLATE`.
s	This attempts to sync all your mounted filesystems, committing unwritten data to them.

Command key	Function
t	This dumps a list of current tasks and their information to your console.
u	This attempts to remount all your filesystems as read-only volumes.
v	This causes the ETM buffer to dump (this is ARM-specific).
w	This dumps all the tasks that are in an uninterruptable (blocked) state.
x	This is used by xmon on ppc/powerpc platforms. This shows the global PMU registers on SPARC64.
y	This shows global CPU registers (this is SPARC64-specific).
z	This dumps the `ftrace` buffer.
0 - 9	This sets the console's log level, controlling which messages will be printed. The higher the number, the more the output.

See also...

For more information about SysRq and systemd, refer to the following page: `https://github.com/systemdaemon/systemd/blob/master/src/linux/Documentation/sysrq.txt`

Red Hat has a complete crash dump guide at `https://access.redhat.com/documentation/en-US/Red_Hat_Enterprise_Linux/7/html/Kernel_Crash_Dump_Guide/index.html`.

Using ABRT

ABRT (**Automatic Bug Reporting Tool**), is a set of tools that help users detect and analyze application crashes.

How to do it...

First, we'll install the necessary packages and then take a look at how to use these tools.

Installing and configuring abrtd

Let's install `abrt` and get it running:

1. Install the `abrt` daemon and tools via the following command line:

```
~]# yum install -y abrt-cli
```

2. Now, enable and start the `abrt` daemon through these commands:

```
~]# systemctl enable abrtd
~]# systemctl restart abrtdThere's more...
```

Using abrt-cli

List all detected segmentation faults by executing the following command:

```
~]# abtr-cli list
```

Here's what the output should look like:

```
~]# abrt-cli list
id 5152056f1c0294cfacf3da09cc09bf062c9dca0a
Directory:      /var/tmp/abrt/ccpp-2015-10-31-14:41:41-10289
count:          2
executable:     /usr/bin/sleep
package:        coreutils-8.22-11.el7
time:           Sat 31 Oct 2015 02:41:41 PM CET
uid:            0
Run 'abrt-cli report /var/tmp/abrt/ccpp-2015-10-31-14:41:41-10289' for creating a case in Red Hat Customer Portal
~]#
```

The displayed location contains all the information about the segmentation fault. You can use this to analyze what went wrong, and if you need help from Red Hat, you can use `abrt-cli report` to report to Red Hat Support.

There's more...

When your RHEL 7 system is registered with a satellite, all bugs will automatically be reported to the satellite system.

You can install additional plugins to automatically report bugs in the following ways:

▶ to Bugzilla (`libreport-plugin-bugzilla`)

▶ via ftp upload (`libreport-plugin-reportuploader`)

▶ to Red Hat Support (`libreport-plugin-rhtsupport`)

▶ to an `abrt` server (`libreport-plugin-ureport`)

Besides the basic bug reporting, you can also create automatic bug reports for Java by installing the `abrt-java-connector` package.

See also

For more information on how to use the abrt tool, refer to `https://access.redhat.com/documentation/en-US/Red_Hat_Enterprise_Linux/7/html/System_Administrators_Guide/ch-abrt.html`.

Auditing the system

The Linux audit system allows you to track security-related information about your systems. It allows you to watch security events, filesystem access, network access, commands run by users, and system calls.

How to do it...

By default, audit is installed as part of the core packages. So, there's no need to install this.

Configuring a centralized syslog server to accept audit logs

Perform these steps to set up the `syslog` server:

1. On the `syslog` server, create a `/etc/rsyslog.d/audit_server.conf` file containing the following:

```
# Receive syslog audit messages via TCP over port 65514
$ModLoad imtcp
$InputTCPServerRun 65514
$AllowedSender TCP, 127.0.0.1, 192.168.1.0/24
$template HostAudit, "/var/log/audit/%$YEAR%%$MONTH%%$DAY%-
%HOSTNAME%/audit.log"
$template auditFormat, "%msg%\n" local6.*
?HostAudit;auditFormat
```

2. On the `syslog` server, restart `rsyslog`, as follows:

   `~]# systemctl restart rsyslog`

3. On the client, create a `/etc/rsyslog.d/audit_client.conf` file containing the following:

```
$ModLoad imfile
$InputFileName /var/log/audit/audit.log
$InputFileTag tag_audit_log:
$InputFileStateFile audit_log
$InputFileFacility local6
$InputFileSeverity info
$InputRunFileMonitor local6.* @@logserver.example.com:65514
```

4. Next, on the client, restart `rsyslog`, as follows:

```
~]# systemctl restart syslog
```

Some audit rules

You can use the following command to log activity on `/etc/resolv.conf`:

```
~]# auditctl -w /etc/resolv.conf -p w -k resolv_changes
```

You can execute the following commands to log all the commands executed by root:

```
~]# echo "session    required pam_tty_audit.so disable=* enable=root" >> /
etc/pam.d/system-auth-ac
```

```
~]# echo "session    required pam_tty_audit.so disable=* enable=root" >> /
etc/pam.d/password-auth-ac
```

Showing audit logs for the preceding rules

You can search for the audit events that have changed `/etc/resolv.conf` using the preceding rule by executing the following command:

```
~]# ausearch -k resolv_changes
```

Here's what the output should look like:

To check all the commands executed by root today, you can run the following:

```
~]# aureport --tty -ts today
```

Here's what the output should look like:

```
~]# aureport --tty -ts today
TTY Report
===============================================
# date time event auid term sess comm data
===============================================
1. 10/31/2015 15:57:27 484 0 ? 7 bash "less /var",<backspace>,<backspace>,<backspace>,<backspace>,<backspace>,<ba
ckspace>,<backspace>,<backspace>,<backspace>,<backspace>,<backspace>,<backspace>,<backspace>,<backspace>,"aurepor
t --tty -ts today",<ret>
2. 10/31/2015 15:57:40 488 0 ? 7 bash <up>,<up>,<ret>
3. 10/31/2015 15:57:39 486 0 ? 7 bash "ls",<ret>
4. 10/31/2015 15:58:57 490 0 ? 7 bash "cat /etc/pass",<tab>,<backspace>,<backspace>,<backspace>,<backspace>,"m/pa
ss",<tab>,<tab>,<tab>,<backspace>,<backspace>,<backspace>,<backspace>,<backspace>,<tab>,"pass",<tab>,<tab>,<tab>,
"o",<tab>,<tab>,"-",<tab>,<up>,<down>,<up>,<ret>
5. 10/31/2015 15:59:13 492 0 ? 7 bash <up>,<ret>
6. 10/31/2015 15:59:15 494 0 ? 7 bash <up>,<ret>
7. 10/31/2015 15:59:54 496 0 ? 7 bash <up>," >> au",<tab>,<backspace>,<backspace>,<backspace>,<backspace>,<backsp
ace>,<backspace>,<backspace>,<backspace>,<backspace>,<backspace>,"root.txt",<ret>
~]#
```

See also

For more in-depth information about audit, refer to `https://access.redhat.com/documentation/en-US/Red_Hat_Enterprise_Linux/7/html/Security_Guide/chap-system_auditing.html`.

10

Monitoring and Performance Tuning

In this chapter, I'll explore the following topics:

- ▶ Tuning your system's performance
- ▶ Setting up PCP – Performance Co-Pilot
- ▶ Monitoring basic system performance
- ▶ Monitoring CPU performance
- ▶ Monitoring RAM performance
- ▶ Monitoring storage performance
- ▶ Monitoring network performance

Introduction

Monitoring your infrastructure is an important aspect of your environment as it teaches you much about its behavior. It will tell you where your bottlenecks are and where room for improvement is. In this chapter, we will monitor performance and not create triggers when certain metrics exceed specific values.

Tuning your system's performance

Companies buy the best hardware their money can get, and they want to use everything optimally. However, it's not just the hardware that makes your applications run faster. Your OS will also behave differently under specific circumstances.

Tuned is a set of tools and a daemon that tunes your system's settings automatically depending on its usage. It periodically collects data from its components through plugins, which it uses to change system settings according to the current usage.

How to do it...

In this recipe, we'll ask tuned which profile to use and apply it through the following steps:

1. First, run the following command to install the required packages:

   ```
   ~]# yum install -y tuned
   ```

2. Enable and start tuned by executing the following commands:

   ```
   ~]# systemctl enable tuned
   ~]# systemctl restart tuned
   ```

3. Have tuned guess the profile to be used via the following:

   ```
   ~]# tuned-adm recommend
   virtual-guest
   ```

4. Finally, apply the recommended profile to tuned, as follows:

   ```
   ~]# tuned-adm profile virtual-guest
   ```

There's more...

You can find the system's tuned profiles used in /lib/tuned/. When you create your own, create them in /etc/tuned in the same way as they are organized in /lib/tuned. I do not recommend creating new profiles in /etc/tuned with the same name as in /lib/tuned, but if you do, the one in the /etc/tuned directory will be used. It is better to create a new one with a different name, including the one you want to modify, and then make the necessary changes in your new profile.

Every profile has a directory, which contains a set of files controlling the behavior of your system. If you explore the `tuned.conf` files in these directories, you will see that these files define the exact settings that other tools (such as **cpufreq**) need to be configured on and that some profiles include other profiles. For instance, if you create a profile for, say, a laptop that is a little better on the battery by applying the `powersave` CPU governor, you could create a new file located at `/etc/tuned/laptop/tuned.conf` containing the following:

```
#
# laptop tuned configuration
#

[main]
include=desktop

[cpu]
replace=1
governor=powersave
```

When you know the bottlenecks of your systems, you can find out how to mitigate them by configuring your system in a specific way. Tuned can come in handy to create and apply profiles based on the performance monitoring of your components.

See also

For more information about tuning your system, refer to the Red Hat Performance Tuning guide at `https://access.redhat.com/documentation/en-US/Red_Hat_Enterprise_Linux/7/html/Performance_Tuning_Guide/index.html`.

Check out the man pages of *tuned (8)*, *tuned-adm (8)*, *tuned-main.conf (5)*, and *tuned.conf (5)* for more information.

Setting up PCP – Performance Co-Pilot

Over the years, a lot of tools have been created to troubleshoot performance issues on your systems, such as `top`, `sar`, `iotop`, `iostat`, `iftop`, `vmstat`, `dstat`, and others. However, none of these integrate with each other, some are extensions to others, and so on.

PCP seems to have a couple of things right: it monitors just about every aspect of your system, it allows the centralized storage of (important) performance data, and it allows you to use not only live data, but also saved data among others.

How to do it...

In this recipe, we'll look at both the "default" setup and "collector" configuration, which allows you to pull in all the performance data you want.

The default installation

This is the basic setup of PCP:

1. Let's install the necessary packages; run the following command:

```
~]# yum install -y pcp
```

2. Now, enable and start the necessary daemons, as follows:

```
~]# systemctl enable pmcd
~]# systemctl enable pmlogger
~]# systemctl start pmcd
~]# systemctl start pmlogger
```

3. If you want to have the system monitored by a central collector, execute the following:

```
~]# firewall-cmd --add-service pmcd --permanent
```

The central collector

Each host that is to act as a collector requires additional configuration. Here's how you can do this:

1. Add a line per system to collect data from /etc/pcp/pmlogger/control, as follows:

```
<hostname> n n PCP_LOG_DIR/pmlogger/<hostname> -r -T24h10m -c
config.<hostname>
```

Here, `<hostname>` is the FDQN to this host. Take a look at the following example:

```
guest.example.com n n PCP_LOG_DIR/pmlogger/guest.example.com -r
-T24h10m -c config.guest.example.com
```

2. After adding a host in this way, you need to restart the pmlogger daemon. Execute the following command line:

```
~]# systemctl restart pmlogger
```

There's more...

By default, PCP logs information every 60 seconds. If you want to increase this and want to gather performance statistics every 30 seconds, you need to change the line starting with `LOCALHOSTNAME` and add `-t 30s` at the end.

Modifying the statistics you gather is a bit more difficult. You can find the configuration for `pmlogger` in `/var/lib/pcp/config/pmlogconf/`. Every file in this directory contains information about which pointers to gather. The syntax is not very hard to understand, but it is complex to explain. The *pmlogconf (1)* man page contains everything you need to know.

If you want to visualize the data on a host, you need to install `pcp-gui`, as follows:

```
~]# yum install -y pcp-gui dejavu-sans-fonts
```

This package comes with a tool called `pmchart`, which allows you to create graphics with the data collected by PCP. The fonts are needed to properly display the characters.

See also

For more information about PCP and its components, refer to their online manuals, which you can find at `http://www.pcp.io/documentation.html`.

Monitoring basic system performance

We need to keep an eye out on global system values. The ones that are particularly of interest are the following:

- `kernel.all.pswitch`
- `kernel.all.nprocs`
- `kernel.all.load`

How to do it...

I'll show you a way to display both text-based and graphical output. Here are the steps:

1. Display live data for the metrics with a 1-second interval for the `guest.example.com` host by executing the following command:

```
~]# pmdumptext -H -t 1 -i -l kernel.all.pswitch kernel.all.nprocs
kernel.all.load -h guest.example.com
```

```
~]# pmdumptext -H -t 1 -i -l kernel.all.pswitch kernel.all.nprocs kernel.all.load -h guest.exampl
e.com
             Source    guest.  guest.  guest.  guest.  guest.
             Metric    switch  nprocs    load    load    load
               Inst       n/a     n/a  1 minu  5 minu  15 min
             Normal      0.00    0.00    0.00    0.00    0.00
              Units       c/s    none    none    none    none
Sun Nov  1 21:34:37         ?   0.16K    0.00    0.01    0.05
Sun Nov  1 21:34:38     55.12   0.16K    0.00    0.01    0.05
Sun Nov  1 21:34:39     64.99   0.16K    0.00    0.01    0.05
Sun Nov  1 21:34:40     54.00   0.16K    0.00    0.01    0.05
Sun Nov  1 21:34:41     69.00   0.16K    0.00    0.01    0.05
Sun Nov  1 21:34:42     53.00   0.16K    0.00    0.01    0.05
Sun Nov  1 21:34:43     67.01   0.16K    0.00    0.01    0.05
Sun Nov  1 21:34:44     53.00   0.16K    0.00    0.01    0.05
Sun Nov  1 21:34:45     75.99   0.16K    0.00    0.01    0.05
Sun Nov  1 21:34:46     61.00   0.16K    0.00    0.01    0.05
```

2. Create a configuration file for `pmchart` to display live data called `system.conf` with the following contents:

```
#kmchart
version 1


chart style plot antialiasing off
        plot color #ffff00 metric kernel.all.pswitch
chart style plot antialiasing off
        plot color #ffff00 metric kernel.all.nprocs
chart style plot antialiasing off
        plot color #ffff00 metric kernel.all.load instance "1
minute"
        plot color #ff924a metric kernel.all.load instance "5
minute"
        plot color #ff0000 metric kernel.all.load instance "15
minute"
```

3. Next, use `pmchart` to plot a live chart for `guest.example.com` via the following command:

```
~]# pmchart -h guest.example.com -c system.conf
```

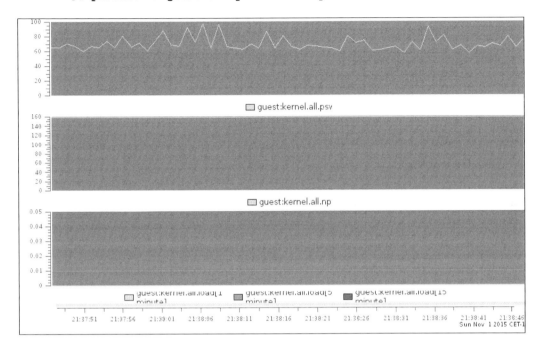

There's more...

The preceding examples are based on "live" data; however, you're not limited to live data. You could increase the interval of `pmlogger` in order to get more data about a troublesome system and then take a look at the generated data afterwards. With other tools, you'd have to use additional tools through cronjob and so on, while PCP allows you to do both.

Here's how you can do this:

1. Show the the data of `guest.example.com` for November 1, 2015 between `15:30` and `16:30` with a 5-minute interval via the following command:

    ```
    ~]# pmdumptext -H -t 5m -i -l -S @15:30 -T @16:30 kernel.all.
    pswitch kernel.all.nprocs kernel.all.load -a /var/log/pcp/
    pmlogger/guest.example.com/20151101
    ```

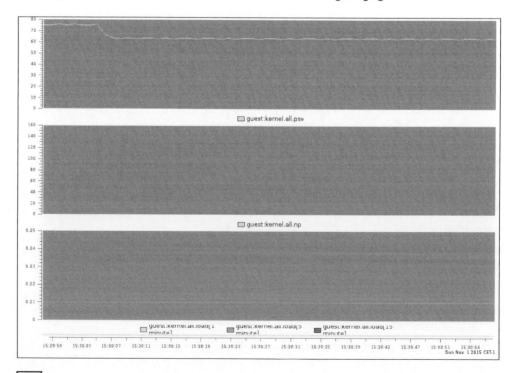

2. You can do the same with `pmchart`, as follows:

    ```
    ~]# pmchart -a /var/log/pcp/pmlogger/guest.example.com/20151101 -c
    system.conf -S @15:30 -T @16:30 -W -o output.png
    ```

Monitoring CPU performance

This recipe will show you how to visualize using `pmchart` and command-line tools to monitor your CPU's performance. We will have a look at the following metrics:

- `kernel.all.cpu.wait.total`

- `kernel.all.cpu.irq.hard`

- `kernel.all.cpu.irq.soft`

- `kernel.all.cpu.steal`

- `kernel.all.cpu.sys`

- `kernel.all.cpu.user`

- `kernel.all.cpu.nice`

- `kernel.all.cpu.idle`

How to do it...

This will show you how to create the text and graphical representation of performance data. Perform the following steps:

1. Display live data for the preceding metrics with a 1-second interval for the host, `localhost`. Execute the following command:

    ```
    ~]# pmdumptext -H -t 1 -i -l kernel.all.cpu.wait.total kernel.all.
    cpu.irq.hard kernel.all.cpu.irq.soft kernel.all.cpu.steal kernel.
    all.cpu.sys kernel.all.cpu.user kernel.all.cpu.nice kernel.all.
    cpu.idle -h localhost
    ```

```
~]# pmdumptext -H -t 1 -1 -l kernel.all.cpu.wait.total kernel.all.cpu.irq.hard kernel.all.cpu.irq
.soft kernel.all.cpu.steal kernel.all.cpu.sys kernel.all.cpu.user kernel.all.cpu.nice kernel.all.
cpu.idle -h localhost
               Source      localh   localh   localh   localh   localh   localh   localh   localh
               Metric       total     hard     soft    steal      sys     user     nice     idle
               Normal        0.00     0.00     0.00     0.00     0.00     0.00     0.00     0.00
               Units         util     util     util     util     util     util     util     util
Sun Nov  1 21:45:55              ?        ?        ?        ?        ?        ?        ?        ?
Sun Nov  1 21:45:56           0.00     0.00     0.00     0.00     0.07     0.20     0.00     3.69
Sun Nov  1 21:45:57           0.00     0.00     0.00     0.00     0.04     0.16     0.00     3.78
Sun Nov  1 21:45:58           0.00     0.00     0.00     0.00     0.05     0.21     0.00     3.71
Sun Nov  1 21:45:59           0.00     0.00     0.00     0.00     0.05     0.18     0.00     3.73
Sun Nov  1 21:46:00           0.00     0.00     0.00     0.00     0.04     0.12     0.01     3.79
Sun Nov  1 21:46:01           0.00     0.00     0.00     0.00     0.04     0.13     0.00     3.81
Sun Nov  1 21:46:02           0.00     0.00     0.00     0.00     0.03     0.13     0.00     3.81
Sun Nov  1 21:46:03           0.00     0.00     0.01     0.00     0.04     0.15     0.00     3.79
Sun Nov  1 21:46:04           0.00     0.00     0.00     0.00     0.04     0.13     0.01     3.78
Sun Nov  1 21:46:05           0.00     0.00     0.00     0.00     0.05     0.17     0.00     3.75
Sun Nov  1 21:46:06           0.00     0.00     0.00     0.00     0.05     0.16     0.03     3.61
Sun Nov  1 21:46:07           0.00     0.00     0.00     0.00     0.09     0.16     0.00     3.62
Sun Nov  1 21:46:08           0.01     0.00     0.00     0.00     0.05     0.16     0.00     3.74
Sun Nov  1 21:46:09           0.00     0.00     0.00     0.00     0.06     0.14     0.00     3.62
Sun Nov  1 21:46:10           0.00     0.00     0.00     0.00     0.07     0.13     0.00     3.72
^C
~]#
```

2. Create a configuration file for `pmchart` to display live data called `cpu_stack.conf` with the following contents:

```
#kmchart
version 1

chart style stacking antialiasing off
        plot color #aaaa7f metric kernel.all.cpu.wait.total
        plot color #008000 metric kernel.all.cpu.irq.hard
        plot color #ee82ee metric kernel.all.cpu.irq.soft
        plot color #666666 metric kernel.all.cpu.steal
        plot color #aa00ff metric kernel.all.cpu.user
        plot color #aaff00 metric kernel.all.cpu.sys
        plot color #aa5500 metric kernel.all.cpu.nice
        plot color #0000ff metric kernel.all.cpu.idle
```

You will notice that I don't use all the metrics in the graph as some of the metrics are combined with one another.

3. Use `pmchart` to plot a live chart for `guest.example.com`, as follows:

```
~]# pmchart -h guest.example.com -c cpu_stack.conf
```

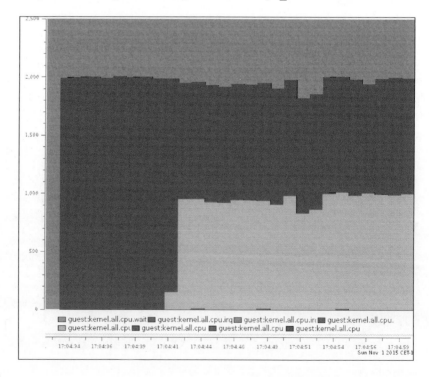

Monitoring RAM performance

To monitor RAM performance, I am only interested in a couple of metrics, not all the memory-related ones. Take a look at this list:

- ▸ `mem.util.used`
- ▸ `mem.util.free`
- ▸ `mem.util.bufmem`
- ▸ `mem.util.cached`
- ▸ `swap.free`
- ▸ `swap.used`
- ▸ `swap.pagesin`
- ▸ `swap.pagesout`

How to do it...

This recipe will explain you how to create text-based and graphical outputs:

1. First, display live data for the preceding metrics through this command:

   ```
   ~]# pmdumptext -H -t 1 -i -l mem.util.used mem.util.free mem.util.
   bufmem mem.util.cached swap.free swap.used swap.pagesin swap.
   pagesout -h guest.example.com
   ```

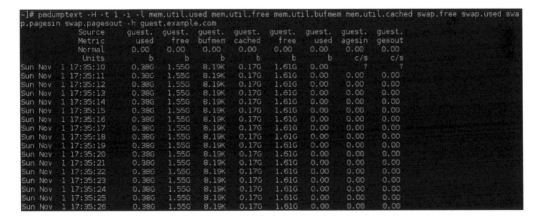

2. Create a configuration file for `pmchart` to display live data called `memory.conf` with the following contents:

```
#kmchart
version 1

chart style stacking
        plot color #ffff00 metric mem.util.used
        plot color #ee82ee metric mem.util.free
chart style stacking
        plot color #ffff00 metric swap.used
        plot color #0000ff metric swap.free
chart style plot antialiasing off
        plot color #19ff00 metric swap.pagesin
        plot color #ff0004 metric swap.pagesout
```

3. Now, use `pmchart` to plot a live chart for `guest.example.com` by executing the following command line:

```
~]# pmchart -h guest.example.com -c memory.conf
```

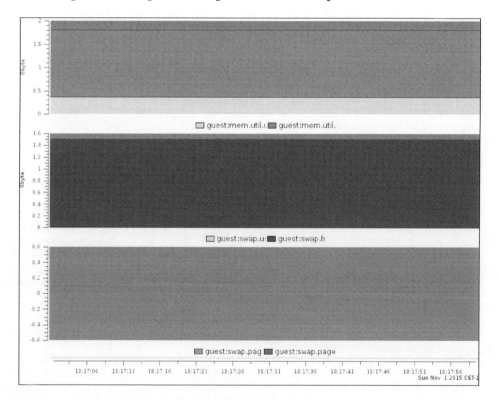

I haven't included the buffer and cached memory in this graph as it's part of the memory-used metric.

Monitoring storage performance

In this recipe, we'll look at the following metrics:

- ▶ `disk.all.read`
- ▶ `disk.all.write`
- ▶ `disk.all.read_bytes`
- ▶ `disk.all.write_bytes`

How to do it...

Let's create a text and graphical representation of the performance data through the following steps:

1. Display live data for the preceding metrics; you can use the following command for this:

   ```
   ~]# pmdumptext -H -t 1 -i -l disk.all.read disk.all.write disk.
   all.read_bytes disk.all.write_bytes -h guest.example.com
   ```

```
~]# pmdumptext -H -t 1 -i -l disk.all.read disk.all.write disk.all.read_bytes disk.all.write_bytes -h guest.exam
ple.com
                  Source    guest.   guest.   guest.   guest.
                  Metric      read    write   _bytes   _bytes
                  Normal      0.00     0.00     0.00     0.00
                   Units       c/s      c/s      b/s      b/s
Sun Nov  1 19:57:13             ?        ?        ?        ?
Sun Nov  1 19:57:14          0.00     0.00     0.00     0.00
Sun Nov  1 19:57:15          0.00     0.00     0.00     0.00
Sun Nov  1 19:57:16          0.00     0.00     0.00     0.00
Sun Nov  1 19:57:17          0.00     0.00     0.00     0.00
Sun Nov  1 19:57:18          0.00     1.81     0.00     0.93K
Sun Nov  1 19:57:19          0.00     0.00     0.00     0.00
Sun Nov  1 19:57:20          0.00     0.00     0.00     0.00
Sun Nov  1 19:57:21          0.00     0.00     0.00     0.00
Sun Nov  1 19:57:22          0.00     0.00     0.00     0.00
Sun Nov  1 19:57:23          0.00     0.00     0.00     0.00
Sun Nov  1 19:57:24          0.00     0.00     0.00     0.00
Sun Nov  1 19:57:25          0.00     0.00     0.00     0.00
Sun Nov  1 19:57:26          0.00     0.00     0.00     0.00
Sun Nov  1 19:57:27          0.00     0.00     0.00     0.00
Sun Nov  1 19:57:28          0.00    29.00     0.00    14.97M
Sun Nov  1 19:57:29          0.00    76.91     0.00    39.52M
Sun Nov  1 19:57:30          0.00     0.00     0.00     0.00
Sun Nov  1 19:57:31          0.00     1.99     0.00    20.40K
Sun Nov  1 19:57:32          0.00     0.16K    0.00    79.95M
Sun Nov  1 19:57:33          0.00     2.00     0.00     0.32M
Sun Nov  1 19:57:34          0.00     0.00     0.00     0.00
Sun Nov  1 19:57:35          0.00     0.00     0.00     0.00
Sun Nov  1 19:57:36          0.00     0.00     0.00     0.00
Sun Nov  1 19:57:37          0.00     0.00     0.00     0.00
Sun Nov  1 19:57:38          0.00     0.00     0.00     0.00
Sun Nov  1 19:57:39          0.00     0.00     0.00     0.00
Sun Nov  1 19:57:40          0.00     0.00     0.00     0.00
Sun Nov  1 19:57:41          0.00     0.00     0.00     0.00
Sun Nov  1 19:57:42          0.00     0.00     0.00     0.00
Sun Nov  1 19:57:43          0.00     0.00     0.00     0.00
Sun Nov  1 19:57:44          0.00     0.00     0.00     0.00
^C
~]#
```

2. Next, create a configuration file for `pmchart` to display live data called `disk.conf` with the following contents:

```
#kmchart
version 1

chart style stacking
        plot color #ffff00 metric mem.util.used
        plot color #ee82ee metric mem.util.free
chart style stacking
        plot color #ffff00 metric swap.used
        plot color #0000ff metric swap.free
chart style plot antialiasing off
        plot color #19ff00 metric swap.pagesin
        plot color #ff0004 metric swap.pagesout
```

3. Now, use `pmchart` to plot a live chart for `guest.example.com`, as follows:

```
~]# pmchart -h guest.example.com -c memory.conf
```

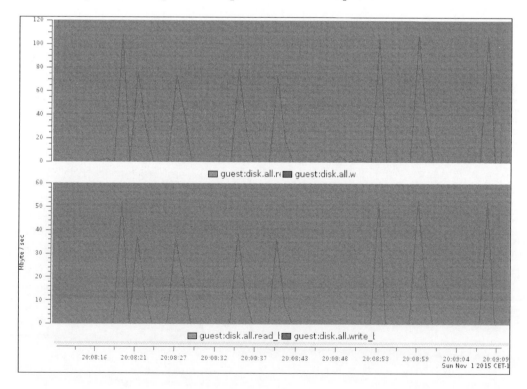

Monitoring network performance

In this recipe, we'll look at the following network metrics:

- `network.interface.collisions`
- `network.interface.in.bytes`
- `network.interface.in.packets`
- `network.interface.in.errors`
- `network.interface.in.drops`
- `network.interface.out.bytes`
- `network.interface.out.packets`
- `network.interface.out.errors`
- `network.interface.out.drops`

How to do it...

Now, one last time, we'll look at how we can create a text and graphical representation of data. Perform the following steps:

1. Display live data for the preceding metrics; run the following command:

   ```
   ~]# pmdumptext -H -t 1 -i -l network.interface.collisions network.
   interface.in.bytes network.interface.in.packets network.interface.
   in.errors network.interface.in.drops network.interface.out.
   bytes network.interface.out.packets network.interface.out.errors
   network.interface.out.drops -h guest.example.com
   ```

2. Create a configuration file for `pmchart` to display live data called `network.conf` with the following contents:

```
#kmchart
version 1


chart style plot antialiasing off
        plot color #ff0000 metric network.interface.collisions
instance "eth0"
chart style plot antialiasing off
        plot color #00ff00 metric network.interface.in.bytes
instance "eth0"
        plot color #ff0000 metric network.interface.out.bytes
instance "eth0"
chart style plot antialiasing off
        plot color #00ff00 metric network.interface.in.packets
instance "eth0"
        plot color #ff0000 metric network.interface.out.packets
instance "eth0"
chart style plot antialiasing off
        plot color #00ff00 metric network.interface.in.errors
instance "eth0"
        plot color #ff0000 metric network.interface.out.errors
instance "eth0"
chart style plot antialiasing off
        plot color #00ff00 metric network.interface.in.drops
instance "eth0"
        plot color #ff0000 metric network.interface.out.drops
instance "eth0"
```

3. Next, use `pmchart` to plot a live chart for `guest.example.com` via this command line:

```
~]# pmchart -h guest.example.com -c network.conf
```

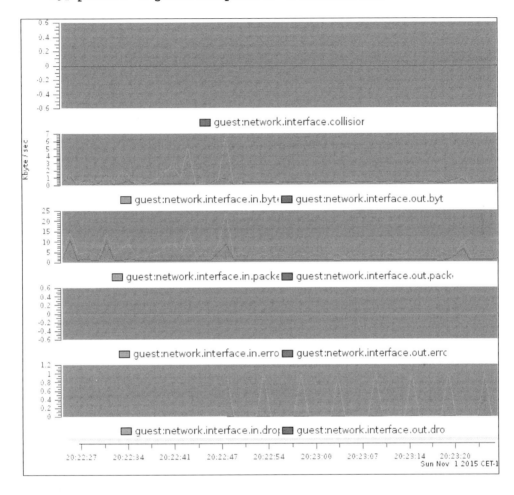

Index

Thank you for buying
Red Hat Enterprise Linux Server Cookbook

About Packt Publishing

Packt, pronounced 'packed', published its first book, *Mastering phpMyAdmin for Effective MySQL Management*, in April 2004, and subsequently continued to specialize in publishing highly focused books on specific technologies and solutions.

Our books and publications share the experiences of your fellow IT professionals in adapting and customizing today's systems, applications, and frameworks. Our solution-based books give you the knowledge and power to customize the software and technologies you're using to get the job done. Packt books are more specific and less general than the IT books you have seen in the past. Our unique business model allows us to bring you more focused information, giving you more of what you need to know, and less of what you don't.

Packt is a modern yet unique publishing company that focuses on producing quality, cutting-edge books for communities of developers, administrators, and newbies alike. For more information, please visit our website at www.packtpub.com.

About Packt Open Source

In 2010, Packt launched two new brands, Packt Open Source and Packt Enterprise, in order to continue its focus on specialization. This book is part of the Packt open source brand, home to books published on software built around open source licenses, and offering information to anybody from advanced developers to budding web designers. The Open Source brand also runs Packt's open source Royalty Scheme, by which Packt gives a royalty to each open source project about whose software a book is sold.

Writing for Packt

We welcome all inquiries from people who are interested in authoring. Book proposals should be sent to author@packtpub.com. If your book idea is still at an early stage and you would like to discuss it first before writing a formal book proposal, then please contact us; one of our commissioning editors will get in touch with you.

We're not just looking for published authors; if you have strong technical skills but no writing experience, our experienced editors can help you develop a writing career, or simply get some additional reward for your expertise.

Hybrid Cloud Management with Red Hat CloudForms

ISBN: 978-1-78528-357-4   Paperback: 174 pages

Build, manage, and control an open hybrid cloud infrastructure using Red Hat CloudForms

1. Understand the infrastructure management capabilities through monitoring and tracking techniques.

2. Control the hybrid cloud infrastructure using policies and define actions based on events and conditions.

3. Learn to view and use trends in the hybrid setup to perform capacity planning and optimization.

Learning RHEL Networking

ISBN: 978-1-78528-783-1   Paperback: 216 pages

Gain Linux administration skills by learning new networking concepts in Red Hat Enterprise Linux 7

1. Discover how to deploy the networks services Chrony, Network Time Protocol (NTP), Domain Name System (DNS), and Dynamic Host Configuration Protocol (DHCP).

2. Deploy RHEL 7 into your Microsoft Active Directory Domain to utilize Single-Sign in Linux and Active Directory with a single account.

3. Master firewalling your network and server with Firewalld.

Please check **www.PacktPub.com** for information on our titles

14971097R00139

Printed in Great Britain
by Amazon.co.uk, Ltd.,
Marston Gate.